Praise for *Cle*

Sue's book is like a great buffet, 50 wonderful helpings from which to choose. If you feel stressed and overwhelmed, Sue motivates you to action and gets you moving toward a life of more focus and success. Sue is America's Leading Authority on Clearing Clutter.

—**Brian Tracy**, best-selling author, speaker, entrepreneur, president, Brian Tracy International

If your life, home or business is full to bursting, pick up a copy of Sue's great book *Clear Your Clutter: 50 Ways to Organize Your Life, Home or Business So You Can Become More Calm, Focused & Happy*. Sue Crum gets people into action with her wit, wisdom, and wonderful ideas. She helps people focus on what's important and inspires them to take action so that they can lead more focused and productive lives.

—**Patty Aubery**, president, The Jack Canfield Companies

Here is a step-by-step guide for reinventing one's life so that it has clarity, calm, and less clutter. Sue Crum is witty and wise and inspires us to achieve more, be more, and create more—all leading to better fulfillment and purpose.

—**Kathleen Seeley**, president, TSG, The Seeley Group Consulting, Inc.

If you're ready to clear your clutter so you can become better organized, more productive, and more focused, then read and absorb the strategies in this brilliant book by my friend, Sue Crum! Sue is America's Leading Authority on Clearing Clutter! Her strategies have the power to change lives.

—**James Malinchak**, featured on ABC's hit TV show, *Secret Millionaire,* founder, www.BigMoneySpeaker.com

Clear Your Clutter has practical wisdom with easy-to-implement strategies. Sue inspires people in a witty and wise way to examine their lives and create more focus and calm.

—**Jill Lublin**, international speaker and best-selling author of three books, including *Guerrilla Publicity* (www. PublicityCrashCourse.com/freegift)

This is a must-read for anyone feeling stressed out today. Sue motivates people with tips and techniques for gaining control of your life so you can be more focused and less stressed.

—**Michelle Prince**, America's Productivity Coach (www. MichellePrince.com)

This is more than a book. It is like having a real live coach by your side, helping you to clear clutter and reorganize your physical space and your calendar. The suggestions and solutions may look simple and practical but they are powerful. Sue shows you how small, specific actions can transform your life to more success and joy-filled tomorrows. Sue is America's Leading Authority on Clearing Clutter.

> —**Jack Canfield**, co-creator, #1 *New York Times* best-selling book series *Chicken Soup for the Soul®*, author of *The Success Principles,* star of the hit movie *The Secret*

This is the **must have** book for those of us feeling stressed, overworked or just plain dissatisfied with various aspects of our lives. Sue has simple yet powerful strategies to get us into action and get things done. I know that I will recommend this great resource to my clients and audiences, and suggest that you check it out, too.

> —**Sharon Worsley**, CEO and founder of The 4 Diamond Leader, author of *The 4 Diamond Leader – How to Wake Up, Shake Up and Show Up in Business and Life*

Clear Your Clutter is a book offering specific strategies that can bring others to focus, productivity, and calm. Sue Crum inspires and motivates people to change for the better with her wit and wisdom. She is America's Leading Authority on Clearing Clutter, and her unique humor and common sense will keep you captivated throughout the entire book.

> —**Elizabeth Hagen**, speaker, author, coach
> www.ElizabethHagen.com

Sue Crum has a way of helping you see your time, your life and your value differently. Listen to her and things get better—FAST!

> —**Jonathan Sprinkles**, TV personality, voted National Speaker of the Year (www.GetAndStayMotivated.com)

This book is packed with specific strategies to help those feeling overwhelmed and stressed. Sue Crum shows you how to look at your world, regain control, and create the future you deserve beginning now. Sue is America's Leading Authority on Clearing Clutter.

> —**Alex Kajitani**, California Teacher of the Year, author of *Owning It*

There may be 50 ways to leave your lover, but Sue Crum has written the 50 ways to calm, happiness, and peace. In her book, she outlines in detail ideas and tips for getting your space, your home and your place of work in real order for real results. Keep this book within arm's reach at all times and refer to it often. You'll be glad you did!

> —**Mark LeBlanc**, owner Small Business Success, author of *Growing Your Business* and *Never Be the Same*

Sue has given a gift to those who have trouble setting priorities—what's wonderful is that it's a <u>menu</u>—you can start anywhere and achieve immediate satisfaction! This book is a fun, great read for anyone interested in clearing up their stuff of life.

> —**Stuart E. Gothold, EdD**, retired LA County superintendent of schools, clinical professor emeritus, University of Southern California

Sue Crum has come up with a surefire method to solve all the world's problems—well, maybe not the world's problems but certainly what is bugging most of us. I defy anyone to read through this book and not begin to see their immediate surroundings in a new light. No stress—just easy steps to better organization and a better life.

> —**Mike Krauss**, president, Total Secure Shredding, Inc.

If you've been waiting for just the right time to get organized, this is the book for you. Sue shows you how to break away from the stuff that is holding you back from being happier with more success and purpose.

> —**Dr. Kent Pollock II**, president, The Chiropractic Center

It's time to get on with the life you deserve and want. Sue will get you moving toward this dream. She is America's Leading Authority on Clearing Clutter. As a full-time firefighter and professor, sometimes maintaining organization can be challenging. Implementing these strategies has already helped me to save time and energy, resulting in more production.

> —**Darren Hall**, captain, Coronado Fire Department, college professor

Sue's techniques and tools can help even the most stressed get better focus and productivity, along with balance in our lives. She offers specific strategies to get us focused on improving the one life we have! Her book is full of practical tips and tools for those on overload and overwhelm.

> —**Wanny Hersey**, superintendent, Bullis Charter School

Sue's new book, *Clear Your Clutter*, contains several gems of advice on how to remove the debris from your business and personal life. A must-read, this book can transform your life one week at a time. If you're looking to get a fresh start, Sue's book is for you.

> —**Richard Villasana**, CEO, Finding Families in Mexico

Special Free Gift from the Author

FREE Organizing Package
Get Started Today!

- Free Quick Start Guide – *Simple Strategies for Clutter Clearing You Can Do Now!!*

Plus

- Free Newsletter – *Quick eTips News for Energized and Efficient People*

Go To
ClearYourClutterCoach.com

Sign Up Now

Clear Your Clutter

50 Ways to Organize Your Life, Home or Business
So You Can Become More Calm, Focused & Happy

Sue Crum

RED Team Press

Published by the RED team
P.O. Box 1061
Carlsbad, CA 92018
For information contact books@RedTeamPress.com

Cover design by Dawn Teagarden

Limits of Liability and Disclaimer of Warranty
The author and publisher shall not be liable for your misuse of this material. This book is strictly for informational and educational purposes.

Warning – Disclaimer
The purpose of this book is to educate and entertain. The author and/or
publisher do not guarantee that anyone following these techniques, suggestions, tips, ideas, or strategies will become successful. The author and/
or publisher shall have neither liability nor responsibility to anyone with
respect to any loss or damage caused, or alleged to be caused, directly or
indirectly by the information contained in this book.

Printed in the United States of America
23 22 21 20 19 18 17 16 15 14   1 2 3 4 5

ISBN-13: 978-0-9903150-0-1
ISBN-10: 0-9903150-0-2
Library of Congress Control Number: 2014910527

For Robert
who continues to be "the wind beneath my wings"

Contents

Part Three: BUSINESS

Acknowledgments

For as long as I can remember I have always held published authors in high esteem. Thanks to the following who have encouraged me along the way to join these ranks: my beautiful, intelligent daughter, Melin, my husband's "crummy" relatives who have accepted me with all my warbles, and my first writers group, Stride Writers (Joy, Alice, Anna, and Karla). A sincere appreciation to my attendees at my speaking presentations, and my organizing and staging clients who have opened their homes and lives to me.

Special thanks for the encouragement from Jack Canfield, James Malinchak, and Elizabeth Hagen. All three of them are speakers, entrepreneurs and published authors whom I hold in high regard.

A big thank you to my awesome assistant, Andrea Hayft, who worked tirelessly and continuously to get this book across the finish line. You have a great eye!!

None of this book or my life's journey would have been possible without the ongoing support of my husband, Robert, who has stood beside me every step of the way.

All of you have inspired me to put down on paper what I believe in my heart.

Preface

Welcome to *Clear Your Clutter*! Thanks for picking up this book. There must be a reason you did, so let me ask you: "What in your life needs de-cluttering?"

For some of us our lives have become way too full, choked to death with too many responsibilities, too many events on our calendars, and too many things in our homes. Whatever the reason, I'm glad you stopped in; stay a moment, flip through this book, and see what resonates for you.

You can start to read at any chapter that is calling to you. The book does not need to be read in sequence, unless you want to do so. However, if you don't know where to start, the beginning is a great option.

My number-one goal is to help you get on with the life you imagine and deserve, whether that's a home you absolutely love, a career that feeds your soul as well as your bank account, or a life that fits just right for you right now.

Step one is DECIDING you don't want to continue on the path you're on.

Step two is COMMITTING to make some changes starting today.

Step three is, as Nike tells us, "JUST DO IT" or, as Yogi Berra so aptly put it, "When you come to a fork in the road, take it."

Here's your fork:

Part One: LIFE

1. Life Balance Wheel and the Mexican Fisherman

Life isn't about waiting for the storm to pass...
It's about learning to dance in the rain.

VIVIAN GREENE

How's your life going right now? This very minute? Not the breezy, easy answer you give to family and friends passing by. Not the curt, short "Everything's great" or the "Wow, I'm so busy" response. The real response. Get your pen ready!

Life Balance Wheel

How content are you in each area of your life? Think of the *outside* of the circle as **completely satisfied** and the edge of the inner circle as **dissatisfied**.

Put a dot on each line where your level of contentment is TODAY. After all areas have been rated, connect the dots with a line.

How does your Wheel of Life look?_____

_____

The area(s) that's working well in your life right now is

_____

The reason(s) it is working well is _____

What's not working? _____

Why? _____

To get your life more in balance you need to spend more time

_____

_____

Today's date is _____.

One month from today is _____(date)

What could you de-clutter this month to get you started on a life that is more balanced?

_____

_____

Four to six weeks from now complete the Life Balance exercise again, using a *colored pencil*, and record the date completed.

Ideally, do this three or four times a year, using a different color each time and recording the date.

Your wheel should start to look in better balance as you clear your clutter from your life, home or business.

The Parable of the Mexican Fisherman

A boat docked in a tiny Mexican village. An American tourist complimented the Mexican fisherman on the quality of his fish and asked how long it took him to catch them.

"Not very long," answered the Mexican.

"But then, why didn't you stay out longer and catch more?" asked the American.

The Mexican explained that his small catch was sufficient to meet his needs and those of his family. The American asked, "But what do you do with the rest of your time?"

"I sleep late, fish a little, play with my children, and take a siesta with my wife. In the evenings I go into the village to see my friends, have a few drinks, play the guitar, and sing a few songs. I have a full life."

The American interrupted, "I have an MBA from Harvard and I can help you! You should start by fishing longer every day. You can then sell the extra fish you catch. With the extra revenue you can buy a bigger boat."

"And after that?" asked the Mexican.

"With the extra money the larger boat will bring, you can buy a second one and a third one and so on until you have an entire fleet of trawlers. Instead of selling your fish to a middle man, you can then negotiate directly with the processing plants and maybe even open your own plant. You can then leave this little village and move to Mexico City, Los Angeles, or even New York City! From there you can direct your huge new enterprise."

"How long would that take?" asked the Mexican.

To which the American replied, "15 to 20 years."

"And after that?" the Mexican asked.

"Afterward? That's when it gets really interesting," answered the American, laughing. "When your business gets really big, you can start selling stocks and make millions!"

"Millions? Really? And after that?"

"After that you'll be able to retire, live in a tiny village near the coast, sleep late, play with your children, catch a few fish, take a siesta with your wife, and spend your evenings drinking and enjoying your friends."

Know where you're going in life. You may already be there.

2. What Is Clutter and How Did We All Get So Much?

The real truth…is that there is only one person responsible for the quality of the life you live. That person is you.

Jack Canfield

A problem can't be solved until we clearly define it and examine its causes.

Clutter comes from the word *clot,* meaning a mass or lump. As our families have gotten smaller and for many of us our homes have gotten larger, clutter (and how to get rid of it) has become a real issue. How could this have happened?

Anna Quindlen, author and former columnist with *Newsweek,* wrote that we have moved into being an acquisitive society. Not inquisitive, but acquisitive. When we couldn't find something, we would head out to the store or order online "another one," whatever that might be: another stapler, another brown belt, or another kitchen mixer.

The reason we picked up another was because we couldn't find the first one. Often, time was an issue, and getting another seemed like the easiest thing to do.

Until…one day when we discovered more stuff did not make us merrier and did not lead us to happiness, but was making us miserable instead.

Clutter comes in many forms: physical clutter, mental clutter, and emotional clutter. Sometimes it's quite visible and noisy. Our home containers fill up to bursting, choking the life out of us and all who are living in that space.

It can also be mental clutter. I call this "clatter chatter." This kind of clutter is the voices in our head, constantly telling us our "shoulds": You **should** be doing this. You **shouldn't** be doing that. **Why** did you do that? Don't forget you **have to** _____ (fill in the blank). You know you have a list running around in there. It's exhausting trying to remember it all and keeping up with that nagging "should" voice.

Others of us have emotional clutter. We're stuck, clotted up, because of events from the past or fear of moving forward. We can't let go of any yesterdays: people who've done us wrong, purchasing mistakes we've made along the way, or items from past relationships gone south that we won't let go of for a variety of reasons.

Some of us are living in the future, saving possessions for distant future events. When I get back to size 8, when I have time to return to tennis, skating, skiing—you fill in the blank.

What clutter is choking you? _____

_____

How long has this been going on? _____

_____

Are you ready to kick-start some action and get de-cluttering your life FAST?

_____

3. Start Small to Create BIG Changes

A journey of a thousand miles begins with a single step.

LAO-TZU

We really can't organize a better life until we clear up the clutter in the life we are in. My goal for you is to start; just begin. What's been gnawing at you? What's the "clatter chatter" been about? What part of your life is so full you are about to burst? Don't make it a three-car garage or a move across the country. Start with one phone call you've been putting off, one junk drawer, one decision you've been delaying for way too long.

That's your starting point.

Make a decision on which small area of your life will be your starting gate.

Write it here: _____

When will you do this? This is KEY to your success.

_____

How much time do you estimate it will take?

_____

What small reward will you give yourself when this is completed?

_____

"Oh, the Places You'll Go" from here!

9

4. Not Time Management but YOU Management

It's one day—half a day, really. I mean you subtract showers and meals. It's like twenty minutes. It will go by like that.

JERRY SEINFELD

We are all trying to squeeze more time into our daily living. Stop someone on the street and ask, "How are you?" and the first thing they say is "Oh, I'm so busy", and then listen to them go on and list a million things they're doing or feel they should be doing.

Guess what?

We all get the same number of hours each week: 168. Time is really the great equalizer. No one, including presidents of countries, gets any more than 168.

The challenge becomes how are we expending those 168 hours? Quick—get a pen and fill in the blanks:

Activity	Hours For Your Activities
Sleeping (Average 50-60 hours)	
Personal care (bathing, grooming, getting dressed) (Average 10-15 hours)	
Meal preparation, eating, and kitchen clean up (15-25 hours)	
Television, internet surfing, e-mail, social media updates	
Commuting, errands, work, and meetings (varies depending on your current lifestyle)	
Add the Hours and Enter Your Total Here	
Subtract That Total from 168 - Result is time remaining available for you	

When I had a client do this math problem, she was amazed at where her time was going. It helped her understand why she was never getting to those bigger projects she desired. Bits and pieces of time were being frittered away on tasks that she admitted were really just busywork.

Once she dumped those tasks from her to-do list, she created blocks of time and scheduled them with the next logical steps to move her projects forward.

So, how did you do with this math problem?

_____

How much time do you really have each week?

_____

Since every minute spent is time we can never get back, what is it you really want to do with the rest of your life? What have you dreamed of doing? What do you *really* want to be doing?

Write those dreams here. _____

_____

What great excuses have you used for why you're not doing your dreams?

_____

What could you take out of your 168 hours right now that would give you some minutes or hours each week to get started on the life you deserve?

_____

When will you do that? _____

_____

Put the date and time you will start here, and transfer that to your calendar/planner.

_____

5. Deadlines Are Delicious

Goals are dreams with deadlines.

DIANA SCHARF HUNT

If it wasn't for the deadline of April 15 I don't think any of us would take time out to send the IRS a report of our financial life along with some money or a request for a refund, now would we?

The concept of Thanksgiving would probably never have taken hold if Abraham Lincoln hadn't established the fourth Thursday of November a national holiday of gratitude and thanks. If it had been left to individual households to just ask the family over any day they'd like to celebrate the gifts and blessings of the previous year, do you think busy families would actually be able to agree on a date, time, and location to do this?

I doubt it.

Without giving ourselves deadlines we fall into the trap of "any day will do." But what often happens is the right day never arrives. The circumstances don't come together. The stars simply don't line up correctly.

That's what makes deadlines so delicious.

We have to trick ourselves and our minds into our own arbitrary deadlines and hold ourselves accountable.

How about looking great for that high school or college reunion? Now there's a deadline many can relate to putting into action.

Getting ready to go on a trip—business or pleasure? We tend to get so much done the 48 hours before the trip starts we amaze ourselves with productivity. The e-mails get answered; the pets get taken care of; the laundry gets done; the house gets tidy; the hair gets cut; the desk gets cleared.

See what I mean?

Set some arbitrary deadlines for yourself. Write them down. Hold yourself accountable and pretend, for just a moment, the plane is taking off 47½ hours from now.

Amaze yourself with what you can get done and get going.

Where will you start? _____

13

Where can you pretend you're going?

_____

_____

What will you accomplish in the next 47½ hours that you have
been ignoring lately?

_____

_____

6. Your Calendar Is King!

Prior proper planning prevents poor performance.

UNKNOWN

Just checking in: You do have a calendar/planner system in place, yes? If you answered no, that you're just keeping it all in your head, that's one *big* headache! It's waaay too much pressure. Our brains were made for creative thought, wonderful daydreaming, and living in the moment with those we love. Let tools assist you in keeping your mind de-cluttered from all those appointments, meetings, and must-dos.

There are many products out there from which to choose. Some folks want the latest technology, and that's great—*if* you have set aside some time to learn its features or you are a quick study in tech toys. When your spouse or best friend tells you to get the latest and greatest tool because he or she loves it, it doesn't mean it is right for you. Build on your strengths and your best learning style. There is no one size that fits all. This is a trial and error process; think of Goldilocks and the different soups and chairs she tried until she found ones that fit just right!

Get your calendar synced with your phone so you do not overbook.

Others have one big calendar on the wall in the kitchen for all to see. That's great—but since you can't take your kitchen with you when you are out, you may end up overbooking. Perhaps at one appointment someone wants to schedule a follow-up. With no calendar with you, you are just guessing at dates or calling them back when you get home to the kitchen, a loss of productive time.

Itty, bitty calendars are not enough. These are given away at card stores, but the squares are so small there's only enough room to write in a doctor's appointment and such. Your life is much bigger than that.

If you are in need of a written planner, check out www.planner-pads.com. These planners are not available in stores and come in different sizes so you can get one that fits with your life right now. Also, the planners can start in January, April, July or October. There is no need to wait until New Year's Day to begin getting organized and planning your best life!

What's important here is to not let the medical appointments and other people's agendas rule your day, because one day turns into the next, and days turn into years. Ask yourself what your plans, your dreams, and your goals are, and get those onto your calendar.

Is your calendar so packed that there is no breathing space for you? Stand back like Google Earth™ looking down on your calendar and life. Is every square filled? Is every person you know placing demands on you?

Are there groups you joined that no longer serve you? Volunteer events that are leaving your emotional tank empty? Have you become unable to "Just Say No"?

REFLECT on your calendar. If a stranger looked at it, what would it say about you?

_____

_____

Crown yourself the king or queen of your calendar and see where you can begin to take back control.

When will you do that? _____

_____

Which activities are you ready to de-clutter? Letting go of what's not working creates space for new opportunities and new beginnings.

_____

_____

If you've been storing dates and reminders inside your gray matter, when will you stop that and utilize a calendar/planning system?

_____

7. Perish Procrastination

Only put off until tomorrow what you are willing to die having left undone.

PABLO PICASSO

Is one of your problems procrastination?

Have you been *thinking about* clearing clutter and getting organized for a long time?

Have you been *talking about* clutter-clearing?

Have you purchased several organizing books for years, but haven't gotten around to reading them or implementing the steps after reading them?

Many of us suffer from this syndrome.

I call it the "Scarlett O'Hara" syndrome:

"I'll think about it tomorrow."

And when tomorrow arrives, we decide there's another tomorrow, and then another.

We rationalize our behavior.

We have more excuses than a 9-year-old with incomplete homework.

We find other projects, other people, other activities to get us headed in a different direction.

How to overcome this?

Ask yourself the following:

Do I procrastinate about everything or just certain things?

_____

_____

Is it disinterest or lack of skill, or do I feel I do not have enough time to get the task done perfectly so why start?

_____

_____

Is the task so big or so unpleasant that it is creating stress and overwhelm?

_____

_____

Steps:

Step 1. Delegate any tasks that someone else could do or simply eliminate the tasks completely.

Step 2. Prioritize what remains and identify a 30-minute block of time when you will focus on an action that could move this project forward. What you are doing here is not looking at the entire elephant and trying to eat the elephant all at once. Just find the place where it makes most sense to take a bite, and then another.

Step 3. Stop at the end of 30 minutes and schedule the next 30-minute block when you will go back to this. Maybe it will be immediately following or maybe it will be another day. The important thing is the commitment to yourself of _when_ you will return to that task.

Step 4. Be sure to schedule in 10–15 minutes of break after each hour or two of a focused session. Give yourself a reward, such as a walk around the block, a call to a friend, or a 15-minute mini-nap. Just don't do all three; pick one!

Step 5. Repeat the cycle above. After several rounds you will find that by getting into the project it was not as bad as you first assumed. Work to increase your work sessions, and that elephant will get eaten one bite at a time!

8. Embrace Simple Pleasures Again

*Let your boat of life be light, packed with only what you need—
a homely home and simple pleasures.*

JEROME K. JEROME

As children our lives were fairly simple and uncomplicated. Along the way they became cluttered with responsibilities, obligations, and demands. Let's go back and relish in the joy and happiness simplicity could bring us once again. Ask yourself:

When was the last time you:

Went for a walk?

Watched a sunset?

Saw a sunrise?

Observed children at play?

Called a good friend?

Sat outside at a café?

Made lemonade?

Hugged someone?

Did something for someone else, just because?

Did something special for another without taking credit?

Wished on a star?

Looked for a rainbow?

Danced?

Sang?

Painted or played?

One of my clients was working from home but had so much work to do she never seemed to be able to escape from it. Before she began working with me, when she was reaching her breaking point, she would fall into retail therapy.

You know—retail therapy: I don't like the life I'm in right now so I'll go buy something to make me feel better. This client did this so

19

often, just for the thrill of the moment, not to purchase an item of clothing for a specific event.

When she contacted me it was at a point where she didn't want to continue this vicious cycle. So many of the clothes she had purchased still had all the tags on them. This wonderful woman decided what would make her feel good was releasing these purchases to a charitable agency that could use them.

Once we did that, the relief and pleasure on the client's face were looks of peace and productivity. She was proud of her decisions and ready to make a list of simple pleasures she could do instead of shop.

There were hobbies she wanted to get back to and family members she wanted to see more often. No longer was she going to escape to fill what was lacking in her life with retail therapy!

We've all gotten so busy, so wrapped up in the next thing, whether that is buying a tricked-out toy, over scheduling ourselves into a stupor of exhaustion, or working to keep up with the folks next door.

It's time to go back to a little deep breathing and realization that some of the best life experiences cost no money at all.

Take another look at the list at the beginning of this chapter. Add to the list pleasures you've thought of that get you living a simpler, less-cluttered life and write them here:

_____

_____

_____

Which one will you do first?

_____

When?_____

Put that on your calendar now.

9. Saying No the Right Way

Put on your own oxygen mask first.

FLIGHT ATTENDANTS' INSTRUCTIONS

Are you one of those who can't say "no"?
Do you get caught up in thinking that there's no one else doing it, whatever the "it" is?

Are you so flattered you've been asked to do the task that you decide, "Well, I must be the only one _____ (qualified, capable, or willing) enough"? You fill in the sentence with what fits you.

Give yourself the 24-hour "I'll have to get back with you" speech.

What is that, you ask?

Here's how it works:

A person asks you to _____.
(Put in any task, committee, event, etc.)

Step 1.   Take a deep breath.

Step 2.   Smile your widest smile (even if you're on the phone). This works even for e-mail.

Step 3.   Ask any clarifying questions so that you are 100% clear on what the person has nominated you for or thinks you'd be perfect at or is begging you to help with. This is an important step. Without it you don't have a complete understanding about the request.

Step 4.   Respond by saying: "Thank you very much for thinking of me for this project, etc. I'll have to give this some thought when I have a chance. I'll get back to you tomorrow." Then give a specific time when you will reconnect.

Step 5.   Get off the phone or on to another topic immediately. Don't keep hashing it over and being wishy-washy. You need time to process away from the inquirer/convincer.

Step 6.   Sleep on it and wake the next day with a clear direction you want to go. If you are going to say "no," you might think of one or two people who might be a better fit for this task.

Step 7.   Contact the inquirer from the day before. If you don't know what to say, a simple "Thanks again for thinking of me. I'm not able to add that to my schedule at this time. However, I was thinking perhaps _____ or _____ might be available. I think either of them would be a perfect fit."

Step 8.   Get off the phone.

Step 9.   Take a deep breath and smile!

10. Our Habits Become Habitual

Successful people aren't born that way. They become successful by establishing the habit of doing things unsuccessful people don't like to do. The successful people don't always like these things themselves; they just get on and do them.

THOMAS JEFFERSON

Are you keeping company with some habits that are no longer serving you well? By that I mean have parts of your life become a bit of a rut, or have a sameness to them? You lament that you aren't getting things done, that you have no time to do the things you want to do, that your time is spent looking for things you've misplaced or going to activities you no longer enjoy. Does this sound like you?

Declare you are putting an end to those habits beginning now.

This is often easier said than done.

The research on habits indicates that we should replace an old habit with a new, better habit.

For example, if you're a smoker and you're ready to clear that clutter—that habit—from your life, often people have success by chewing gum as they are releasing cigarettes from their world. Though some might say chewing gum isn't good for you, it's much better than smoking cigarettes. Smokers are used to something in their mouths so there is a need to replace that activity with something similar but safer.

In the past it was thought that 21–30 consecutive days were enough for a new habit to get into our muscle memory. Jerry Seinfeld called this consecutive-day strategy "Don't Break the Chain."

However, in Gary Keller's great book of 2013, *The One Thing,* he cited researchers at the University College of London who spent time in 2009 studying habits and how to make them automatic. Their results suggested that it takes an average of 66 days to acquire a new habit. For easier behaviors it was fewer days and for difficult behaviors more than the 66. Keller suggested not to give up too soon on the new habits you want to develop.

On the following page list some old habits you are ready to clear from your life, and across from each select a new habit you can put in its place.

Old Habit	**New Habit**
_____	_____
_____	_____
_____	_____
_____	_____
_____	_____
_____	_____

With a new habit, strive for *consecutive* days of new behavior for it to take hold in your life. Remember to not break the chain!

Don't worry if you mess up. Just start the count again with the vision of seeing the new habit becoming a part of your new, clutter-free life.

11. Unleashing Unhealthy Habits

The greatest wealth is health.

Virgil

Let's take a look at some habits that may be unhealthy for us. Anything in excess, even if it's legal, could qualify as not good. Here are just a few: alcohol, tobacco, chocolate, sugar, starches, too much couch-potato lifestyle.

Are there some unhealthy habits you would like to unleash? For some of us clearing up the clutter of the pounds that we've added may be the reason we picked up this book in the first place.

The first step in changing behavior is acknowledging there's a problem in the first place. So what's your habit that's not healthy for you?

_____

How long has it been a struggle for you?

_____

_____

_____

What have you tried before, and did it work?

_____

_____

_____

For how long?_____

Why do you think it stopped working for you? What changed?

_____

What's *one step* you could take to put you back toward a path of healthier habits? For example if unhealthy eating is a problem, could you take one of these actions: keeping a food log, planning meals ahead of time, wearing a pedometer and recording steps daily, getting tempting food out of your home, always having healthy snacks available so as not to just grab the first food available, cutting back on fast food and/or meals at restaurants, getting a support group, or getting a free health/fitness app for your smartphone?

List one step you will take here.

_____

When will you begin?

_____

Who could help you and hold you accountable?

_____

What small goal could you set?

_____

How could you reward yourself when you reach it?

_____

_____

Put this commitment in your calendar/planner now.

12. In and Out Days

He is rich who owns the day.

RALPH WALDO EMERSON

For some of you in the western United States, your mouth may have started to water after reading the title of this chapter. I'm not talking about food here, but I sure do love those burgers!

Some of us live in a part of the country where there is a drive-thru/dine-in establishment of tempting delights, and a name like the title above.

I'm not talking about calories, carbohydrates, and clearly dangerous eats. No, I'm talking about our schedules—our calendars.

Many of us have responsibilities that take us out of our homes every day, all day—five, six, or seven times a week. Others of us are making several trips in and out of our homes maybe three to five times each day.

If you own your calendar a little bit more than that, or would like to, listen up.

Just for a moment, picture *you* in charge of determining your destinations and when to go here, there, and everywhere.

Visualize a clean slate of a calendar ahead of you. Maybe it's next week or next month. Maybe it's a clear space for tomorrow.

Put yourself in the driver's seat and decide when you want to leave your nest and where you want to go and what you need to do.

Place those "out" responsibilities on *one* day or part of a day. In other words, when you're out, you're out, and when you're not, you're not.

Gee, maybe there should be a song with that title!

A young mom hired me to help her get organized. She is the CEO of a very busy household, and has a lot of responsibilities and interests. We took time to examine and evaluate her calendar and routine.

What we uncovered was she was doing a lot of running around and spending enormous amounts of time in the car. By switching up several activities, we were able to find larger blocks of time for focused, concentrated projects she had not been able to get to that she really wanted to do.

This one adjustment to her life brought much-needed peace and

27

calm, and also gave her the time blocks to get to projects she desired.

Many of us are expending way too much time running here or there, even if it's in a car. Freeway fiascoes and commuting conundrums often leave us in such a frenzied state we are no good to anyone else, especially ourselves.

What I'm suggesting here is a bird's-eye view of your calendar over the past week or month. Were there times when you made a trip out of the house and then got back home with less than a half hour to spare and then another trip out?

Did some days feel totally lost and nothing got done that you had planned?

My guess is you were going "in and out" waaay too much.

If you can take some ownership of your days, can you block out time to do "in" projects at home—focused, concentrated, super-charged levels of efficient and effective transformation—and then other days when you plan "out" activities?

Gas station, car wash, post office, dry cleaners, bank, meds pick-up, donation drop-off, medical appointments, hair, nails, business meetings, friend for coffee—all those pesky errand events.

Just picture it: you are now in charge of what gets on the calendar and when. Plan your "in" days and "out" days now for next month. Then before making appointments on any day make them on the days you plan to be out.

Your in-home productivity will soar, especially if you are running a home-based business. Your energy will increase, and you will find yourself more at peace and more relaxed because now *you* own the day!

13. Get Yourself an A.P.
(Accountability Partner)

A friend is one that knows you as you are, understands where you have been, accepts what you have become, and still, gently, allows you to grow.

WILLIAM SHAKESPEARE

If you are really serious about clearing up the clutter in your life and moving toward living a calmer, focused and happy life, you need to order up an A.P.—A.S.A.P!

It's a tough road to row it alone. It's so easy to slack off, to change gears, or just to put ourselves in park and become like Scarlett O'Hara (let's just think about all of this tomorrow).

Rather than becoming the queen or king of procrastination like Scarlett, I want you to succeed *this time*.

So this time you need to put in place an accountability partner (A.P.). This person can serve as your cheerleader when you start to beat yourself up that your life and your spaces aren't perfectly uncluttered and serene.

Who could this be?

Anyone who cares about you and will not sabotage your steps toward success.

If one of your clutter-clearing goals is to get rid of unwanted pounds, don't pick a good friend who wants to take you out for a celebration dessert when you lose a few pounds. That person is on a mission to help you *find* those pounds again.

Your A.P. doesn't even have to live near you. This person can be anywhere in the world, but someone who will encourage you, check in with you, and care about your de-cluttering success. This A.P. will not let you totally slack off, once you've made a commitment to change.

Often, it works best if your A.P. is not your spouse. Sometimes sabotage comes to us from our own home when we are told, "Oh, you're not trying to get organized again, are you? That will never work. How long do you think this is going to last this time?"

Sometimes I serve as my clients' A.P. If they have quite a bit of clutter clearing to do, I help them make decisions, celebrate their successes and assist with regrouping during any setback.

Some of my clients are looking for a rapid response approach to clutter clearing. Once they've made their commitment to change, they are eager and ready to reclaim their life and environments as soon as possible. They love having me as their A.P. and love the slight kick in the pants I can give them.

It's important in picking your A.P. to go a bit outside your family/close friend inner circle. You don't have to make any broad announcements of new beginnings and fresh starts. Just quietly begin—with your A.P. listening supportively to your plan of attack through e-mail or a phone call and agreeing to be there to congratulate the wins and help you regroup with any temporary setbacks.

14. Marathon Days Are Marvelous

Get stuff done fast®.

JAMES MALINCHAK

Have you ever run a marathon?

Did you ever think you would?

Well, guess what? It's not *that* kind of marathon.

As you begin to envision a clutter-free lifestyle, home, and/or business, putting a couple of marathon days into your calendar might be just perfect for you to kick-start your new life.

Here's how they work, and you never have to leave your home or office.

You won't end up any fitter than when you started, but your environments and *life* just might be!

1. Think of a buddy you could ask to join you in a marathon. This person does not have to live near you at all. As long as you can communicate by phone, e-mail, or text with this person, that's all you'll need.

2. Tell your friend you plan to do a marathon (or half-marathon) and you're hoping they will do one with you at their place. A full marathon is five-six hours; a half marathon is three hours.

3. You will be at your home or office working on your project and your marathon buddy will be at theirs, working on a project they've been meaning to get to but "just haven't had the time." Tell them you are providing the structure for them to use some of the time they have and get that gnawing project moving toward completion.

4. With calendars at the ready the two of you agree on a particular date. It needs to be the *same date*. Depending on if you're doing a full or half marathon, agree on your start time. It needs to be the *same time*. The time allocated will determine if it's a full marathon (five or six hours) or a half-marathon (three hours). Be clear about start and end times, especially if your buddy is in a different time zone.

5. *Before* the agreed-upon marathon date, each buddy gathers

31

any supplies needed, such as heavy-duty trash bags, recycling bins, banker's boxes, donation bags or bins, manila file folders, hanging file folders, gloves, timer, etc. The needed supplies will depend on what the project is for that designated day.

6. The *day before* the marathon you and your partner communicate. Often, this is best in an e-mail, as then there is a *written* record of the scope of the project. You will write to your buddy about the space or project you'll be working on for your marathon. Outline specifically what you plan to de-clutter and organize. Write out the supplies you have gathered. State your vision of how you want the space to look when you are finished that day. Write how you will reward yourself after the marathon.

7. Your marathon buddy does the same and sends an e-mail your way.

8. This can be done by phone, but is much more powerful in written form as your buddy might think of supplies you've not thought of that will make your project more successful. You may do the same for your buddy.

9. Each buddy obtains protein snacks, water, and a mid-day meal already made or super simple to fix.

10. The *night before* review your supply list, confirm your healthy snacks and water are ready, and make sure your mid-day meal is all set.

11. Get a great night's sleep (at least seven–eight hours).

12. Eat a good breakfast with protein.

13. One buddy phones the other at the start of the marathon. This is a less-than-five-minute phone call! Agree on check-in times for the day. Ninety minutes is a great block of focused time. Synchronize your watches and decide who will make the check-in call in 90 minutes. Announce what specifically you will focus on for the first 90-minute clutter-clearing session.

14. Put your phone away (even under a pillow) so you can concentrate on the task at hand. You may need to let family members know ahead of time that you will not be answering the phone that day as you are doing a marathon. That ought to get them darn curious!

15. No answering the door. No getting the mail. No dog walking.

No surfing the net, checking email, or feeding the cat.

16. Marathon runners stay focused and so can you!

17. Throughout the marathon, check in at 90-minute intervals with quick calls to your buddy. You are there to cheer your friend through their project and they are there, at their end, to be your guide on the side.

18. The last call at the end of the marathon can be longer than the previous short calls. Identify breakthroughs, any challenges, next steps, and rewards.

19. Schedule another marathon day right then for next month or next week.

20. *Celebrate* what you accomplished in less than a day!!

Note: Marathon days can be done with more than two; just stay focused and clear on the day's objectives. If a full marathon seems too overwhelming, begin with a half-day.

15. 911 Emergency

To be prepared is half the victory.

MIGUEL DE CERVANTES

Clutter-clearing one's life has to include preparing for the awful and outrageous possibility that a major disaster could strike you and your family. If our papers, lives, homes, and offices are in such a state of disarray, any emergency could become quite disastrous!

Plan now to organize all the specifics.

Immediately following Hurricane Katrina in September 2005, I signed up for specialized training with the American Red Cross. I was so moved by what I saw on television that Labor Day weekend that I cleared my calendar and requested service with the American Red Cross. First, I worked with families who arrived in San Diego with next to nothing, coming from the hurricane-stricken area.

Next, I was deployed to Louisiana for several weeks. My specific assignment there was to meet with the clients of the disaster, hear their stories, review their paperwork, and help them with rebuilding their lives.

What I heard from all of them will never leave my heart. The pain and suffering were etched into the parents' faces. The children's looks of bewilderment and confusion and the parents' fear of the future were so visible and heartbreaking.

Here are the lessons I learned from that:

1. Establish a Written Family Communication Plan now, including a meeting place at a nearby neighbor's or the local school or church, somewhere away from your house but that the family could walk to and that is well lit.

2. Include in your written plan the name and number of an out-of-town contact, as local phone coverage may be very limited. Everyone memorizes this information.

3. Have recent photographs of each family member.

4. Practice the safest way to escape from your home.

5. Create a plan for your pets.

6. Make grab-and-go bags for each person in the family. Include

such things as bottled water, a lightweight flashlight with batteries, protein bars, a change of clothes, any prescription medicine, and a family photo for each child.

7. Have a first-aid kit for the size of your family.

8. Keep the following ready: cash ($300–$500), picture IDs, passwords, verification of home address, and insurance information.

9. Have an emergency preparedness kit that includes an Eton emergency hand-cranked radio.

10. Have an emergency preparedness kit in each automobile with appropriate supplies depending on the size of your family.

Noah built his ark before the floods arrived.

16. Leftovers, Anyone?
(No Turkeys Involved)

*A lot of things remain unfinished by the end of the day
and likewise remain incomplete by the end of life.*

UNKNOWN

All of us have unfinished business. Perhaps these are promises we've made, like "Oh, I want to have you over for supper soon." Yet, that's as far as the dinner invite goes.

We mean well. We have every intention to make that happen, but life has a way of interrupting. We're waiting for the puppy to grow up, the kids to move out, the baby to not throw food on the floor, or the flooring to get replaced.

We have all sorts of excuses.

Maybe we were in the middle of a big scene at work or at a holiday gathering. Today you recognize that you behaved badly and things were left in the air. You kind of put the whole episode out of your mind, except in a little crevice where you've played the scene over and over but with a different outcome.

Let's get all these leftovers out on the table and schedule some time to address them, one plate at a time.

Taxes not filed? Promises not fulfilled?

What's left over on your table?

List them all here and get them out of your mind and in front of you.

After making a list, go back and in the second column put a date when you will address each one. Schedule those on your calendar now.

What's Eating at Me?	Date I Will Take Action
_____	_____
_____	_____
_____	_____
_____	_____

_____   _____

_____   _____

_____   _____

   Often I do this exercise in my speaking presentations. This is a most powerful activity. People get down on paper some things that have been gnawing at them for a very long time.

   Afterward they thank me for getting clear on what they need to do next to clean up these life leftovers. The closure they reach is extremely powerful and gets them ready to move forward with more peace, productivity and purpose.

17. Lobby for Hobbies

Develop a hobby. The winds of enthusiasm sweep through you.
Live today with gusto.

DALE CARNEGIE

Hobbies—you've got to be kidding! If you've just said those words, you're exactly the prime candidate for a hobby. If you've been filled up with to-dos of your own making or someone else's and you're not enjoying life anymore, think back to the last time you had some fun, doing something that absorbed your mind, stretched your soul, and made you smile from ear to ear.

That's the kind of hobby I'm talking about. Perhaps you used to bake or sew or bird-watch or hike or collect coins. Maybe you remember flying kites, walking dogs left in shelters, knitting blankets for infants in neonatal centers, or volunteering at a food bank.

Then life got busy on you, too busy, too packed.

Is there an activity/hobby you've always wanted to do or you did years back?

The benefits of hobbies are endless. For one thing hobbies give our minds a rest from all the items running around in there we think we should be doing.

When we get really focused on learning a new skill or remembering an old one, we have to pay attention. We have to be in the moment. We can't be wondering and worrying about a million other things.

If we don't steer the boat or thread the needle or decorate the cake with accuracy and attention, well, we are not going to have a successful experience, now are we? By focusing on the task at hand we can lose ourselves in it.

A break from work and worry is often just the refresher course we need. Even God took Sundays off.

Step back from your busy, cluttered life and pick up a hobby or two. Not because you have to, but just for fun and freedom!

What hobby is waiting for your return or is something you've always thought about doing?

When can you put this on a calendar and take a first step?

_____

    Write that date in your calendar now and smile knowing you have something just for fun to look forward to in the coming weeks.

18. The Closing of Each Day

Day is done, gone the sun....All is well, safely rest....

"Taps," scout song at sunset

When I was a Brownie and a Girl Scout, I had the opportunity to attend sleepover summer camp for several years. While each experience was only for two weeks at a time, the eight weeks I spent there over my lifetime have remained as one of my most cherished memories.

We slept on cots with bug netting over our faces so as not to get eaten alive by the many mosquitoes of Michigan. There were four girls to a tent. I so enjoyed hearing about the lives of my tent-mates after lights out. I looked forward to it each evening.

But before that we had to first close the day.

We had a ceremony each evening right at sunset where someone on the bugle would play "Taps" and the chosen girls for that night would bring the American flag down from the flagpole and fold it just so. This was such an honor and privilege; we all worked hard so we could get a turn at closing out the day.

Our ceremony took place right at the edge of the lake—the same lake where we had swimming lessons every day and watermelon races in the water, too.

Where I live now, I am blessed to watch the closing of the day, seeing the sun appear to slide into the Pacific Ocean. This is a big deal here, with everyone out at sunset: dogs, babies in strollers, all kinds of people—young and old, all come out to watch the day close. Some nights a bugle player stands on a ledge at one of the restaurants and plays "Taps" right as the sun makes its final plop into the Pacific. Everyone applauds at the end.

I have taught many of my clients this "closing of the day" routine, and they have found it helps them calm down the chaos of their lives. The steps below give specific solutions to getting at that peace we all deserve. These steps, along with some deep breaths, will set us up for a successful night of sleep.

Create your own close of the day:

1. Slow down any highly charged physical activities for family members. In other words, don't put high-exertion, high-energy

41

tasks at the end of the day.

2. Close the kitchen and announce that it's closed.

3. Get off electronics at least 60 minutes before lights out.

4. Write in a gratitude journal three great things that happened that day.

5. Look at your calendar/planner for the next day's activities and pick out what you'll wear.

6. Start visualizing a wonderful, great day of success coming up tomorrow.

19. Happy 100th Birthday!

*You should live every day like it's your last day
because one day you're gonna be right.*

RAY CHARLES

Congratulations! Let's pretend you've made it to 100. What a great milestone!

Everyone is coming to the celebration tomorrow at your house. The media will be taking videos of the event, and interviewing you about your successes and secrets to living a long, productive life. Neighbors, relatives, and friends near and far will all be in attendance. Some of these folks you've not seen in many years. You're starting to get a little anxious about the event, but nonetheless, there it is on your calendar/planner.

You recall years back when your life was cluttered with too much to do and your home, world of work, and life were so full and packed you thought you were being smothered with stuff.

It's now 20___ and it's hard to believe you're 100. (Write in the year you will turn 100.)

It's been _____ years since you cleared up the clutter in your life and made changes that really helped you get on with the life you wanted to live. Think back to the things, activities, and people you were willing to let go of. What or who were the main items you cleared out of your life?

_____

_____

As you cleared up the clutter that was suffocating you, what were the activities and people you replaced them with that have made you calmer, more enjoyable, and happier to be around?

_____

_____

43

Picture your home and write a description of it before the party gets started. Be sure and include how your clutter-free home makes you *feel*:

_____

_____

_____

_____

What are some goals you have achieved that you had always wanted to do but had never been able to do before?

_____

_____

_____

Happy Special Birthday to You!!

20. S.T.E.P.S.™ to Success
for Clearing Clutter in any Space

Have nothing in your houses that you do not know to be useful
or believe to be beautiful.

WILLIAM MORRIS

Before you jump into Part Two: Home, I want you to take a look from 30,000 feet up. Don't just start tearing apart a room or a multi-car garage without a plan in mind.

I want you to be successful this time, by following these five steps below:

S: **Survey** the space with an outsider's eye, like you are viewing the room for the very first time, and **sort** like items with like. For example, put all the shoes together, all the staplers together, etc. This is the sort and sift phase.

T: **Toss** the obvious: trash, expired coupons, magazines you'll never read, shoes you'll never wear, and old catalogs. This also means to recycle/donate. This is the "pitch and ditch" phase, where you are releasing to the universe items that no longer serve you, but perhaps will be useful to someone else or that belong in another room.

E: **Examine** what's left. Keep the essentials—what really belongs in the space; if possible, empty the space.

P: **Plan** the new space. Draw a sketch of how you'd like the room to be. Use Post-it® notes, so you can move furniture around on paper before physically doing so. This is where you give everything you are keeping a home. Without a home any countertop or any drawer will do, and that's what got us into this mess of clutter in the first place.

S: **Start returning** furniture pieces that are keepers, beginning with the biggest items first. Continue rebuilding the space until you have all the furniture placed. Then add the other items that belong there and only what you want in the space.

With a box at the ready marked "Take to another room" deliver those items now that belong in another part of the home.

Part Two: HOME

21. Home C.H.A.O.S.
(Can't Have Anyone Over Syndrome)

There's no place like home!
DOROTHY (THE WIZARD OF OZ)

Have you been suffering from C.H.A.O.S. for way too long?
**yes** How long? _**years**_
This section will address all home spaces, indoors and out.
Some of us live alone; some of us live with a partner, and some of us reside with others, ranging from a few to many.

Whatever your situation, ask yourself: Am I suffering from C.H.A.O.S. (Can't Have Anyone Over Syndrome)?

can't put things away - starting but not finishing them.

What has this been costing you in friendships, relationships, money spent, and stress?

lots of stress

If this is you, when do you plan to stop the chaos?

now

Why do you think it's a good idea to get out from the chaos?

to be calmer

Picture your home without the chaos. Close your eyes and see its potential. Open your eyes and write what you envision your home environment could be.

How would that new space make you *feel?*

calm

Who would be the first to have over once the chaos has cleared?

Leslie

What's today's date? _6|15|18_

What date will you be inviting a friend or family member over—for tea, for toast, for a terrific treat?

What will you serve?

Where will you and company sit?

What time of day will work best?

Get a picture in your mind of all of that happening. It is possible. Let's begin.

22. Get the Junk Out of Your Trunk

There is no one giant step that does it. It's a lot of little steps.

PETER A. COHEN

A great place to begin clearing clutter in one's living spaces is to start with a project of a doable size. I caution participants in my speaking engagements when they get so energized about the idea of clearing clutter to not go home and tear apart a three-car garage that night.

I want you to be successful. I want you to see that you can do this. I want you to believe in yourself and not get frustrated, feeling like a failure. I want your clutter-clearing experience to be A+.

That's the reason I always say to start out small and build success one project at a time. Start with the junk in your trunk, if you don't know where to begin.

Have you ever pulled into a parking space and noticed the car next to you? Sometimes I don't notice a thing about the car next to me—never giving it more than a fleeting glance, just making sure we'll all have room to return to our cars with ease and no one's car will get scratched or dinged.

Other times I can't help but look as the car is screaming "disaster" as soon as I get out of mine. The dashboard is covered with stuff. The front seats have evidence of every meal for the past several weeks. The back seats are filled to bursting with a little of this and a lot of that.

It gets me thinking about the trunk, imagining what junk could be hiding there.

Could this be you?

Start here.

Get trash bags, recycling bins, a couple of medium-sized boxes, and a timer. Put on some moving music and get clearing quickly.

Set a timer for 60 minutes max and swiftly get the trash out of the trunk, the back seats, the front seats, and the glove compartment, and off the dashboard.

Keep moving and go back through each of those locations in your car, pulling out anything that belongs elsewhere. Label one box "garage" and another "house." If several people live with you, make a box that will go to each of their rooms.

51

Label another box "car." Go ahead. Pull items out that should live in the car and put them in the car box. Keep moving as fast as you can to get the car emptied of everything except the items that were included on the day you purchased it, such as the spare tire and any built-ins.

Get a vacuum with a long hose and extension cord or a powerful hand-held vacuum and rev up the motor—yours and the machine's. Work to beat the clock by moving quickly but thoroughly through the crevices and corners of your car.

If you have any upholstery car cleaner or steering wheel cleaner, apply that next.

Step back and admire your work. The car may not look exactly like it did the day you bought it, but I bet it's looking much better.

Think through what absolutely needs to live in the car. This could be and should be a vehicle first-aid kit and an emergency preparedness kit. You might include CDs you enjoy listening to, but before putting them back loosely, think through a container they can live in for easy access.

What else is essential for you?

Evidence of insurance?

Roadside assistance info?

Car registration?

Cell phone charger?

Sun shades for dashboard protection?

Only return the critical and the crucial to the car.

Have you beaten the time?

I hope so.

Next, return garage items to their homes in the garage or storage space.

Items that should be in the house need to be delivered to their proper rooms.

Put away the vacuum and all supplies and congratulate yourself on a one-hour clutter-clearing job.

Hats off to you! There are plenty of more hours in the day for other activities.

23. Other Places to Begin

*It is better to take many small steps in the right direction
than to make a great leap forward only to stumble backward.*

CHINESE PROVERB

No junk in my trunk, you say? Fabulous. Your car is a container of comfort and function. That's terrific! Where is another small living space where you could start clutter-clearing? Think:

Bathroom drawer

Medicine cabinet

Kitchen drawer

Entryway to house

Front porch

One dresser drawer

One desk drawer

Portion of one countertop

Entryway table

Guest bedroom

Children's bedrooms

A corner of the dining room table

You get the idea.

Think small. Think probable. Think possible.

You can be very successful if you just begin with one of the above.

Grab needed supplies, such as trash bags, recycling bins, a few empty boxes, marker for labeling, and a timer.

If you are doing a drawer, dump the contents of the drawer onto a countertop and quickly separate and sort. Look for immediate items for trash/recycling. Get rid of them. What's to keep? Move quickly, putting like items with like.

After the quick sort, step back and look at what's left. What are the keepers and where do they belong? The reason we end up with multiple junk drawers is because no one knows where anything should live, so any drawer will do.

A client asked me to help with her kitchen junk drawers one day. I asked how many she had, and she started counting. When she got to six, I said, "Let's quickly go in the kitchen and grab some trash bags along the way."

Hers is a busy household of seven people. As she opened each drawer, we both noticed that the six drawers had a lot of similarity in their contents. They were mirrors of each other. When I asked a few questions, it became apparent to both of us that if she wasn't able to differentiate what should go in which drawers, how could the rest of her family?

In less than one hour we had tossed the trash, grouped the great stuff, and assigned specific homes to each drawer. How one uses their spaces is crucial to success. There is not a "one way fits all" solution. What works for her family may or may not work for another.

The secret is assigning a home for each of the categories of items that are remaining. It is best to use a label maker so everyone knows what is contained in each drawer. When any space will do, that's when we end up with multiple junk drawers.

At the end of this experience my client had no junk drawers and was excited to teach her family the new homes for the items remaining in the kitchen.

24. The Best Date Night of the Week
(Even if You're Married)

Success is relative. It is what we can make of the mess we have made of things.

T.S. ELIOT

Got your attention on this one, didn't I?

I'm here to tell you the absolute best date night of the week.

You say you're not dating? You're married? You'll never go on another date?

Makes no difference to me. This date night *is* worth getting ready for.

No special makeup needed.

No beauteous hair-do.

No special outfit.

No money necessary.

And you don't have to drive anywhere or stay out too late!

So what am I talking about?

The absolute, favorite, best date night each week (yes, that's right—*every week*—rain or shine) is...

Drum roll, please ...

The night BEFORE the Trash Man Cometh!!!

Okay, you're asking, what's so special about that?

This is your opportunity—your Golden Ticket, your sweepstakes reward, to make sure you have as many "gifts" ready for him as your area allows.

Start a happy dance around your home the night before his truck is due on your street. Turn on your favorite music. Grab your trash bags and your recycling bins, and have a donate bag at the ready for items your trash man doesn't need.

Put your glasses on and get moving. Look in all the usual places first, but then make another sweep.

Peek in the nooks and crannies of your container (your home) and see what else could go to the waste-management wizard who'll be coming your way tomorrow.

Have a To Donate bag or bin with you as you probably will see some items you are ready to release to the universe, letting others use and enjoy them. With these you can do one of two things immediately when this bag is full: 1. Place in your car and drop off at a donation center next time you have an "out" day or round of errands, or 2. Call your favorite charity and arrange for a pickup date for the following week.

If you decide on #2, calendar in several more rounds of "happy dance" time so you have enough gifts to make the donation agency's stop at your place worth their effort.

For the past 25 years or so many of us have been filling up our containers. Now is the time to take off our rose-colored glasses and see what monster we've been creating.

If you have no idea where to start with clearing the clutter out of your life, the weekly trash man date is as good a place as any to begin.

Get out your calendar now and mark down the night before he cometh in your neighborhood. Block out time to get ready for him. I promise you: Getting gifts for the trash man will get you started on the BEST DATE NIGHT EVER!

25. Consider Consignment

Some of us think holding on makes us strong but sometimes it is letting go.

HERMAN HESSE

Take a look around your home. How cluttered *is* your container, your home?

Is it full to bursting?

Sometimes the first thing we need to do is evaluate how much furniture we have living in each room.

Take a tour and some time to jot down a few notes in a small notebook, not on a loose piece of paper.

Was the furniture purchased for a previous place and you thought it would be okay here?

Was it given to you from others who wanted to clear clutter from *their* lives?

Did you pick it up years ago at a garage sale and say you'd only use it until _____ (the kittens grew up; the dog died; the kids left; the business took off or any other excuse you had)?

Have others commented when they've been over that your home is starting to look like a furniture showroom?

If you answered "yes" to any or all of the above, you should consider consignment as a clear step in the clutter-clearing process.

Having too much furniture in a room can suck the energy out of the space. Take off your rose-colored glasses and really complete the tour of your home with just furniture shopping as your focus.

Which pieces *could* you release to the universe?

Which ones *should* you relinquish?

Many communities have consignment stores. If yours does, drop in and take a look around at the kinds of furniture they accept. The furniture changes all the time as pieces get sold and new ones arrive. Consignment rules may vary, so it's important to find out how your local consignment store works.

The purpose of your trip is not to buy more for your home but to see if this store has items similar to the furniture you want to release. Usually pricing is picked by the folks there. Often there is a 50-50 split with the consignee. The management does not have to take everything, so it's important to find out specifics, including what will happen if your merchandise does not sell.

Many times you can send a photo to see if what you have is something they would be willing to sell in their space. If you are unable to transport the pieces to the store, ask about pickup services for a fee.

After a period of time (usually 30 days or so), if the item has not sold, the management may reduce the price. If it still doesn't sell, then you have the opportunity to pick it up and donate it to your favorite charity or give them the go-ahead to donate it.

There are several reasons why I like furniture consignment stores:

1. They are marketing the items for you and displaying them at *their* place.

2. You are not setting up several appointments at a potential buyer's preferred time and then having no one show up.

3. It is *much* safer for you! There is no need to give your address to total strangers to come over for a look-see at which pieces you are selling.

    And while they are doing their look-see, they might be checking out if you live alone, how far away the nearest neighbor is, what hours you are home or if you are female or frail.

26. Your Bedroom: Your Sanctuary

The pursuit, even of the best things, ought to be calm and tranquil.

MARCUS TALLIUS CICERO

When you come back into your home, after slaying dragons and putting out fires each day, it's most important that there is at least one room in your nest that brings you calm, contentment, and closure to the day.

That room needs to be your bedroom. If you don't know where to start on your new clutter-free lifestyle, the master bedroom is a perfect place.

Here's the easiest, no-brainer way to bring immediate happiness and health to that space:

Make your bed each and every day before breakfast.

Wow! Did I lose some people with this one? Are you busy telling me all the reasons why this is not possible? All the morning responsibilities you have? All the people, big and little, in your home who can't do a thing without your help?

I've heard all of these excuses before, and your morning routine is no better or worse than anyone else's.

Here's what I do know: The bed in our room takes up about 80% of the space. Even if your room looks like a tornado just blew through it, by making the bed a certain level of calm will take over the room.

Granted, your bedroom might not be ready for a magazine cover photo shoot, but it will look 100 times better than leaving the bed totally disheveled.

There is something magical that happens, also. When you pop back in there to get something or to change clothes at the end of a long day out in the world, a little smile will start across your face, and you'll breathe a sigh, and say, "Ah," just thinking of last night's sleep or looking forward to climbing back in bed that night.

The very best is making it before breakfast. If this is some new, radical idea for you to get a hold of, start by promising yourself it will be made before leaving the house, or if you plan to be home that day, as soon as breakfast is finished.

Get a duvet cover if the thought of tucking in this and that is more than you can face in the morning. One quick pulling up of the duvet and you're done!

Once you've mastered this or are already in the habit of bed making, it's time to take a look at the rest of your sanctuary. Is it one?

Do you have so many electronics in there that your room could be mistaken for a big-box tech store?

Are the heaps of laundry everywhere and at this point it's getting difficult to recognize "the cleans" from "the dirties"? When that happens we end up washing everything over because we are just not certain.

Are the items in here ones that belong elsewhere in the house? Children's toys, mail unopened, mail opened but not processed, boxes of stuff, dishes, food, etc.

It's time to schedule a de-cluttering dance for this space.

Gather some boxes and label one of them "take to another location." If you have a lot of stuff to move out, you may need a box for each location (for example: baby's room, garage, kitchen, laundry).

Remove from your sanctuary anything that is not going to bring you peace and pleasure.

Quickly hang up clothes that are not wrinkled.

Put other clothes away in drawers. Do not get into opening all the dresser drawers at this point.

Right now we are working to bring down the volume of the visual noise screaming at you when you are trying to sleep.

Focus on the visible.

Scan the entire room.

Don't forget to look under the bed. Some years back I worked with a client whose space was somewhat small. She was trying to use her bedroom also as her office, and she wanted to establish a craft corner in there as well.

She was really asking the room to do too much. In clearing the space and relocating her office to her dining area, we unearthed gifts from a former boyfriend under the bed. These large art pieces were not particular favorites for the client, and the glass was broken on at least one of them. She commented that she did not even like the piece.

I quickly moved everything from under the bed out of the bedroom. Then we sorted through the items and made decisions about "keepers" and "tossers." Coming up with where keepers will live is key to success on any of these projects.

As you have boxes to deliver to other rooms, set the timer and allow no more than 20 minutes to deliver them to their proper places. If you have family members who have brought their things into your space, round them up and hand out their "gift" boxes.

Take a deep breath and look around.

See your serene sanctuary and start smiling, thinking about a great night of sleep tonight and every night in the future!

27. Clothes Encounters of the Best Kind

Never wear anything that panics the cat.

P.J. O'ROURKE

Life might be easier for all of us if we lived in a nudist colony. Think of the money and time we'd save not having to shop for clothing, no decisions and indecisions on what to wear each day or evening or every time the news changes the weather forecast. No one would have excuses for being late to events with the ubiquitous comment "I had nothing to wear!"

Of course, we might be getting chilly out there, let alone embarrassed. And then think about sticky thighs on those seats in our cars! Yuck!

We come into this world without clothes, and when we leave we won't be bringing much along the way to our next stop. But in between, as we grow up and then, for some of us, grow wide or grow narrow, decisions about what to wear for what can stymie us.

Has your closet taken over? Is it full and bursting? Did it used to be a walk-in closet but you haven't been able to walk in it for some time now? Or do you think all your prayers would be answered if only it was a walk-in closet, and then life would be perfect?

Are your dresser drawers so jammed that lots of time goes into searching for something you're sure is in there somewhere, but just not sure where?

The Pareto Principle really plays out with our clothes. This is the famous 80/20 Rule first mentioned in 1906 by Italian economist Vilfredo Pareto in relationship to the disparity that the majority of land, about 80%, was owned by only 20% of the population. There was no equal relationship; 100% of the people did not own 100% of the land.

Think of that in terms of your own clothes. Open the dresser drawers and closet, and ask yourself: Am I wearing 100% of what I have? If not, reflect on why that is so.

We really tend to wear about 20% of our wardrobes 80% of the time. We have our favorites—our go-to outfits, depending on events and weather. There are certain items of clothing for particular situations, and then there are ones that are just sitting there, in our closets, waiting for us to take them out for a spin! They feel sad, lonely, and neglected. Now is the time to make decisions on those.

The closet can be a great place to clear up clutter. Read all the steps below **before** you begin so you have all the supplies ready for success!

Step 1.   It's best to begin on the floor. Pull everything out and see what's down there. This is the ideal way to really see what you have. Proceed with the rest of the closet. Get it as empty as possible.

Step 2.   Have several large boxes and/or bags and a marker ready. Label them: "keep," "maybe keep," "donate," "toss" (not even good enough for donating), "return," "repair," "laundry," "return to other rooms/people." Sort, sort, sort into these categories. Ask yourself, "Do I love it and wear it?" It is best to try everything on not only to see if it fits, but to see if it fits you and your life *right now.* If you can recruit a friend to join you for this part, that is even better, but make it someone who will be very honest with you and not appease you.

Step 3.   Really take the time to clean the inside of the closet. Wipe down the shelves, and vacuum or sweep/mop the floor. Go deep.

Step 4.   Get rid of plastic dry cleaner bags. They will trap moisture. Start a container of wire hangers, donating them back to your dry cleaners. These wire hangers are not a friend for your clothes.

Step 5.   Now look at the empty space of the closet. Survey each area and decide what can go where. Use Post-its® or blue painters' tape to label where you will put things back into the closet.

Step 6.   Use velvet, slimline hangers. They come in different colors and are now available at many retail stores or online. (I love the black ones! They look most elegant.) These hangers are strong but slender, and the top twists with ease. Put the item back on the hanger, almost with your eyes closed, and then you can switch the top part to make the clothes all line up facing the same way! Save some plastic hangers to use with clothes that are wet. If you like to hang t-shirts, slimline hangers might be too frustrating to use; if so, use plastic ones instead.

Step 7.   Using your designated, clearly marked areas, begin returning the hanging clothes you love and wear. Put like with like: all the blouses or shirts together by color, pants by color and/or style, and dresses—the same way. What we want to do here is create a simple system for retrieving as well as returning quickly so there is no excuse to set it down somewhere else. I love looking at my closet with the colors grouped together. This makes it so easy to find something, instead of hunting all over the place. Get them back in the closet lightest to darkest or with the colors you gravitate to wearing the most at a place of easiest access. Not everyone looks good in every color. Get your colors done or read up on what colors look best with your skin tone, hair, and eyes, and release those items that don't make you look and feel sensational!

Step 8.   Be sure you've categorized all your purses, belts, scarves, and jewelry using the boxes from STEP 2. Any purses you plan to donate need to have extra-focused attention from you to ensure that nothing of value or identification has been left inside. Return all of these items by color and style as well. See what you can hang. Take measurements of spaces before purchasing any hooks or containers.

Step 9.   For shoes, follow the steps above. Read also the chapter titled "If the Shoe Fits, Wear It!" in this book.

Step 10.   Do all of the above with items in drawers. Think like with like. Store out-of-season items in another closet, if possible. Roll t-shirts and place in drawers by color and sleeve length. Do the same with sweatshirts, jeans and workout clothing.

Step 11.   Put "donate" bags in your car or call and schedule a pickup. Remove "toss" and "return to other rooms/people" items.

Step 12.   Congratulations!! You have made it this far. Survey the new spaces with deep breaths. This project can be overwhelming for some, so if it looked big to you, hopefully you worked with a buddy who kept you focused on the task at hand. With a small notebook, see if there are definite holes in your wardrobe. For example, a favorite blue shirt just got released to the universe, but you wear it with so many outfits. Put it on a list and schedule a time to fill that specific void. This gets you to smart buying and intelligent decision-making instead of impulse buying.

Take time to notice if there are any new color or style combinations you had not considered before because you hadn't had breathing room among your clothes to see the new possibilities. In your same notebook, make a list of these or take photos of these "new" combinations, so you don't forget the possibilities.

28. Lingering with Laundry?

Laundry: wash, dry, fold, repeat.

UNKNOWN

Has your laundry gotten the best of you?

Dreaming about your next life and hoping it's on a desert island somewhere in a nudist colony so you won't have to think about laundry?

Well, let's work with the life we have, the one where laundry can get the best of us, even if there aren't many people in the house. I think the main problem with laundry is the Neverland aspect—not like Peter Pan, where you can go if you don't want to grow up. Instead, laundry becomes that constant in one's life, whether living with a large group or living alone. It *never* ends.

Let's say you live alone or with one other person. Yet, every time you turn around you are bumping into a laundry basket—things to fold, things to put away, things to wash, things to iron. (Are you still ironing? I hope not.)

I want you to think back to that children's rhyme:

"This is the day we wash our clothes, wash our clothes, wash our clothes."

Remember that one?

It all made perfect sense. Just assign one day a week and that's it. Wash, dry, fold, and put away all clothes on one day.

Without the discipline of the one-day plan, we get into an any day will do mode so we end up doing laundry all week long and it's out and about *all the time.*

Wait, you say. There are many people in my house. One day a week will never work. All right. Let's set up a schedule.

Anyone 11 and older is quite capable of doing their own laundry.

There, I've said it. Probably made some people angry, but I firmly believe this. There is absolutely zero incentive for children 11 and older to care about their clothes if Laura Laundress is following them around picking up behind them, putting their clothes in the wash, doing all of their laundry, including folding, and putting it away.

Zero incentive.

If I know I don't have to do any laundry, there is absolutely no reason for me to take care of any of my clothes because I know no matter how rolled up they are or where I've dropped them around my room or the house, Mary Maid will come and clear it all up for me.

If you've been doing everything in the laundry arena for everyone and you are worn out, now is the time to reclaim some breathing space for you and do just enough laundry, but not too much.

Call a family meeting and announce you need help in this area of your life and feel a need to resign from this job.

For children 11 and older, have them discuss their extra-curricular schedule and work out which day they can schedule for their laundry. Otherwise, put their names in a bowl and decide which days of the week will be available for them to take care of their own laundry. Announce a day and draw a name. If they don't like the day, let them trade among themselves.

You've just reduced your laundry load; your life is now a little lighter!

Post the schedule where family members can see it. Provide each person with at least one training session on how to work the washer/dryer and let them observe you modeling the correct behavior. Depending on the age and attention span of the individuals, this may take a couple of lessons. The important part is reinforcing positive behavior as they acquire this new skill. Without instruction they will be set up for failure and announce that no one can do the laundry as well as you, and now it's all back in your laundry basket!

Be sure there are one or two laundry baskets in each child's room, or designate space in a laundry room if you are lucky enough to have such.

Baskets without lids work best if you have high expectations for people of any age to use them. If you already have ones with lids, can the lids stay open so family members don't have an extra step to go through to get clothes inside?

Since we are the adults in the home we need to model for the younger ones. If they see how the adults handle where to contain dirty laundry and get it processed efficiently, the children can learn this skill, too.

Examine your laundry dilemma. If it is everywhere all over the house, take back control and block out some time to get back in charge. When we get far behind on laundry issues and we no longer can tell "the cleans" from "the dirties," and no one in the family seems to have clean clothes, that thought of the nudist colony or escaping to a desert isle alone starts to creep into our dreams.

One day the youngsters in our lives will move on or grow up and launch lots of laundry in their own homes. Don't make this an ongoing battle with people you love, but come up with solutions, getting their input, so you are no longer lingering about all the laundry loads!

29. If the Shoe Fits, Wear It!

I did not have 3,000 pairs of shoes; I only had 1,660.

IMELDA MARCOS

Calling all the shoe fanatics out there!

You know who you are.

You haven't met a shoe sale you didn't like (or participate in) yet!

It's time for a little "sole searching."

Are you buying shoes continuously to fill some other void in your life?

Do you keep purchasing shoes because, unlike clothes, no matter what you weigh, your shoe size stays about the same?

If your weight is way more than you wish, do you think everyone is just looking at your feet and then no one will notice that you are 25 pounds or more overweight?

You're dreaming.

If you haven't found time to clear up the clutter in your whole closet, maybe you could take a peek at just the shoes.

Drag them out of every nook, cranny, and corner of your bedroom and closet. All right, maybe they're in other rooms as well. Corral them and put the number of pairs you have here: _____

Now, count how many feet you have and put that number here: _____

Oh, that was a bit mean, wasn't it? I'm sorry. I know you have shoes for this and that, and this outfit and that outfit.

Go ahead and put like with like (all the sports shoes together, all the work shoes together, and so on).

Ask yourself "Are there shoes here that hurt my feet—that I know will give me blisters or headaches just wearing them for 30 minutes or less?"

Can I release these?

Are there shoes that I've hung on to but I know I bought on a whim and have only worn once or twice? Evaluate whether or not you will wear them in the next six months to a year.

Are there specific shoes for an activity you used to do but haven't done in years and have no plans to return to? Can you release these?

There are many people who are not as fortunate as we. Ask yourself, "Could I release some of my shoes to others who need them?" If so, when?

30. Refrigerator Raid and Grocery Shopping

The odds of going to the store for a loaf of bread and coming out with only a loaf of bread are three billion to one.

ERMA BOMBECK

Is grocery shopping a big deal or a little deal at your home? Here are some ways to simplify this necessary event:

1. Order groceries online to be delivered. Check availability in your area.

   Since we tend to order the same kinds of items most weeks, there will be a record of your latest purchases, making reordering a breeze.

2. Have a meal service delivered to you. These have become more popular, with people having less time in the kitchen. In San Diego Pamela Croft, a certified chef and the owner of www.DinnerAtHome-SD.com, offers meal prep and delivery right to you. Catering is an additional service she provides. Individuals on specialized or restricted diets and busy career households can benefit from services like these, especially if preparing meals is not a part of your core genius.

   If you are done with doing dinners, and don't live in San Diego, check out who is in your community who could provide meal service for you.

3. Have a grocery pad on the side of the refrigerator or nearby. You can purchase these at Target or Z Gallerie, or make your own.

   If you shop at the same store each time, you can go down the aisles of the store and record the items you normally get from each section. Leave space for any write-in candidates. In front of each item put a ____ where any family member can put the number of how many are needed. Make a stack of copies (to use one sheet per trip) and as items are used, the person using the last of something is responsible for making

73

sure it gets on the list.

Have room on the sheet for what meals you've planned for the week so it makes it super simple to recall why you bought certain items.

4. Assign groceries to the person who loves to do errands; think about who is best suited for this. While that person is out, someone remaining at home raids the refrigerator for items that can be condensed. How many ketchup bottles do we need to have open at once? What food didn't get eaten and is now past its prime? Any unopened foods that could live in a pantry instead? What you're doing here is making room for the new "guests" to arrive so there will be plenty of seating inside the refrigerator and pantry. Look in the crisper. Are things still fresh or are they floppy? Perhaps it's time to release some of these items or eat them now. With a damp paper towel quickly wipe down as much of the open shelves as possible.

If there are two of you in the household, one person should tidy up the refrigerator, making room for new gifts, while the other is out shopping. Show thanks to the shopper by being the one to put away the purchases

Oops—something forgotten? Just add it right away to next week's list, and realize life will go on and it will be okay to get that next time.

31. The Heart of the Home: The Kitchen

If you can organize your kitchen, you can organize your life.

Louis Parrish

It's been said the kitchen is the heart of the home, so I ask you: How's the pulse of yours?

Is your kitchen a place where it's easy to prepare meals, food is readily available for fixing, there's a place to sit down nearby, and family members know where all the supplies and various foods are stored?

Or is it a catastrophe of calamity where surfaces are covered, the refrigerator is growing things that are starting to move, and the supplies are out on the countertops because there is no room in any drawers or cupboards?

Has the kitchen become the dumping ground for items no one knows what to do with? Mom, this needs to be signed. Important mail—better leave it out where I can see it. No one's had time to grocery shop, so who wants to order something for delivery or pickup?

Do you dream of sit-down meals like Betty Crocker used to make or for someone other than you fixing them?

Have you seen how crowded restaurants are these days? Not just on weekends but every night of the week. Is no one having sit-down meals at home anymore?

Let's clear up the clutter here so that delicious dinners and delightful desserts in a de-cluttered space can be in your near future.

Take off your blinders and take a good, hard look at the kitchen.

Are there dirty dishes out? Wash them or get them in the dishwasher fast.

Next, what else is on the countertops? Papers, magazines, coupons, school assignments? Gather all the paper items and square up their corners (get them all facing the same way and in a neat, tidy stack).

Next, look at the rest of the things on the countertops. What items are sitting there because someone gifted them to you, but you're not using them nor plan to (such as a bread machine, a pasta maker, or a strange ceramic cookie jar)?

75

Just because someone gave you an item for your kitchen does not mean you need to keep it out forever. If it's from your mother-in-law and your relationship is a bit shaky, think about where this could be stored until her next visit. Then, put her to work using it with you.

If it's from other people, evaluate whether or not you've had the item long enough to release it to the universe and donate it to someone else. Only keep appliances and kitchen items you plan to use and love. There is limited real estate in our kitchens, so we need to be smart about allocating prime space to important items we really use.

When the dishwasher is finished, quickly unload it or assign that task to another member of the household, so the machine is ready for loading when that next dirty dish arrives.

Clean the sink until it shines, and step back and admire your work. In just a few short minutes you've made an attack of the heart, but not gotten a heart attack doing it. Job well done!

At the end of each evening meal, set up a routine to get the dishes done and put away as quickly as possible. After the pots and pans have been scrubbed and put away, the countertops cleaned and cleared, and the sink sparkling and shiny, it is time for the evening announcement:

"The kitchen is now closed."

Say this even if you live alone. Use these exact words and state them firmly but friendly. At a family meeting explain that there are hours of operation in the kitchen, just like at a restaurant, and you can no longer afford to stay open 24/7.

Anyone who has the need to eat or drink something after the kitchen is closed is responsible for their dishes, glassware, utensils, and the counters. Resort to paper products if you have to, but keeping your kitchen/restaurant open for 24 hours daily will take your heart out of your kitchen!

32. Who Is in Charge Here?
Home Command Center

What the world really needs is more love and less paperwork.

PEARL BAILEY

Our home should be our castle, our retreat from that outside world that can get mean sometimes. We want our homes to be places of escape and comfort for us, whether we live alone or with others. Creating that respite from the world can often be difficult because of so much paper coming in at us from all sides, reminding us that we really don't live on an oasis.

There are bills to pay, school forms to fill out, events to schedule, and people to contact. At the end of a day the paper seems to fly in and land on the first horizontal space available, often the kitchen counter.

It plops down in the kitchen for many family households because that's where the house manager or CEO of the home is often preparing the evening meal. Children are sharing their day and maybe even showing what forms need to be completed for school, sports, and other activities—that's if you're lucky enough to have them show you these!

When both spouses work outside the home, dinnertime can be the only time the family comes back together, and there can be a lot of stress; everyone wants to be heard and recognized, often at the same moment!

There seems to be little time for relaxation and recuperation during the week. We are quickly onto the next chore and then the next. No wonder we fall into bed at night so exhausted.

Maybe we live alone or with one other, and the cacophony of family living is not going on at our place. Yet, we still feel out of control with the papers piling up.

Let's get you back in control with a command center.

This simple container can get all those papers standing up at attention, vertically, so you can read, review, and release each one as you process it.

How does this work?

Think of the categories of current papers in your specific life.

Here are some general ones:

action

awaiting reply

bills to pay

calls to make

do it now (2 minutes or less)

data entry

events to calendar

e-mails to send

school papers to sign

to read

to file

someday/maybe

school or team rosters

You can also include tabs for specific members of the family or schools the children attend. In addition, consider having a tickler file in the front of your command center with 43 tabs for the 12 months and the maximum number of days in a month, 31. Items that are time sensitive can be placed in the month the event will occur. When that month begins, simply drop that month's items behind the specific dates of those events.

Place the named, hanging files in a vertical file box. Quickly sort through any papers that are on horizontal surfaces and place in the appropriate folder.

After dinner, as you are getting ready to close the kitchen, grab a folder or two and take command, and process its contents quickly!

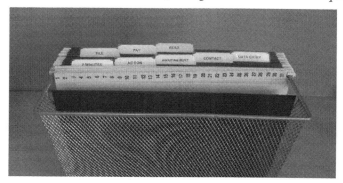

Command Center

33. Bathrooms

A bathroom should be sterile and beautiful and functional.
It should exude Japanese-style purity.

Isaac Mizrahi

Bathrooms can be great places to start clearing clutter. These rooms have specific functions with built-in appliances and cabinetry, and generally can be de-cluttered and organized by a single person. Apply the simple strategy of S.T.E.P.S.™ from Part One to any and all bathrooms, and these spaces can be de-cluttered in no time.

S: **Survey** the entire room as if you were seeing the space for the very first time. Take it all in, letting your vision soak in every corner. Sort like with like: hair products, teeth items, make-up, etc.

T: **Toss** the trash and any obvious outdated items, especially expired makeup. Mascara is one that expires quite fast, after three to six months, so when in doubt, throw it out. Lipstick is good for about one to two years. Foundation lasts about one year, as does nail polish. Eye shadow can last up to three years. Powder can be used about one to three years.

These are simply guidelines. If you notice any changes in smell, texture, or color, it's probably time to release these to the universe and let go.

While you're working on the Toss step, toss all the towels and washcloths into the laundry bin.

Using empty shoe boxes or small plastic containers from the kitchen, you are now ready for the next step.

E: **Examine** what is left in the room. Are there items that belong in other rooms of the house that got dropped in here by you or someone else? Ask yourself: what are the essentials for this space? Empty as much of the room as possible, including the items under the sink in those hard-to-reach areas.

P: **Plan** how you can better utilize the storage areas and what could be the minimum number of things left on the countertops.

S: **Start** returning items only after you have cleaned the bathroom from top to bottom. Bring back larger things first, keeping in mind which items get used most frequently. If you share the space with another, create space for that person's essential items, also.

Add fresh, clean towels and maybe a plant or two to create the perfect oasis in one of the most important rooms of the home!

34. Living Areas

Out of clutter, find simplicity.

ALBERT EINSTEIN

Living areas can be a challenge for many of us because, quite frankly, we are doing a lot of living in these rooms. In many homes there is only one living area. It might be called the living room, the great room, or the family room, but if there is only one, it's important to have storage available so loose items have a home at the end of the day.

We can never get to clutter-clearing and organizing these spaces if there is no place for things to live. When items have not been assigned a home, no one in the family, including ourselves, will put them away because we don't know *where* to put them!

As parents we often say, "Pick up your toys." However, that's not a very clear direction to children; there they are holding their toys and saying they've picked them up. We need to teach them *where* the toys can live and make that access easy for the youngsters to reach. By modeling for them that we have assigned homes for our things and helping them in the beginning find homes for their toys, we are teaching them lifelong habits.

Before the close of the day have a 10- to 15-minute music pickup party built into the schedule, and get everyone involved. Make it into a dance and have some fun with it. If you don't get the children involved, the toys remain out for someone to trip over, or you get to spend the rest of your evening putting their items away, instead of some personal time for you.

If you are lucky enough to have more than one living area, it becomes easier to designate one space for adults or special occasions and the other space a family room.

In either case it's essential that we model the behavior we are expecting from our children. When we take something out and use it, we need to return it to its home when we are finished with it.

Keeping these living areas clutter-free can go a long way in creating family peace. If that is not happening for you, call a family meeting and identify the specific chores that need to occur in these rooms and agree on who is capable of doing each task.

You live alone or just with adults? The same applies to you. Put on some music and end the day with your own pickup routine. In the morning your mind and body will thank you!

And don't forget to dance!

35. Gifts from Others
(Or How Many Pink Pigs Do You Really Need?)

The truly rich are those who enjoy what they have.

YIDDISH PROVERB

Are you a collector? Sometimes in my presentations or with my coaching clients I come across folks who have collections. I ask them to tell me about them.

What emerges is a story of something that started out quite innocently one day, when either the individual thought it would be fun to collect some kind of item, or a friend or relative suggested it.

Perhaps it was on a trip. Maybe it was when the person was young and a grandmother or neighbor started them on a collection.

One.

Two.

Three.

But then three became 13, and 13 became 30, and all of a sudden what seemed to happen overnight is the collection became crowded and cluttered.

Everyone knew about this person's collection so when they were traveling or shopping and saw a pig, a turtle, a butterfly, a toad, a tomato—fill in any word here you like—the purchase was made and presented with "I saw this and thought of you. I know you'll just love it for your collection."

Hard to get out of these collections now, isn't it?

This is where tough love has to kick in.

This is when you have to say, "Enough is enough, and I have enough _____ (fill in the blank)."

You can't keep quiet about this anymore.

First, you have to tell yourself that you don't need any more in your collection to make you happy—that you have plenty. You know while you are admiring your collection, there are people out there making, building, selling, and getting money through their creations of new items for your collection.

Second, you have to ask yourself: are all the ones I currently have artfully and clearly displayed? Or are they in boxes, bins and barrels I can't get to and therefore I'm not able to enjoy them or see them?

Third, how much real estate are they taking up? In other words, have you given a great deal of the real estate in your home to house these stuffed animals, these ceramic seals, these turquoise teapots, or whatever grouping you have?

Fourth, are you spending part of your cleaning routine dusting, cleaning, or polishing these prizes? Sometimes our possessions end up possessing us, instead of the other way around.

Could this be you?

Last, and most importantly, you have to decide from this moment forward that your collection is complete and go public with your decision. That means you let everyone know who has been giving you these gifts that you have stopped collecting and you are not needing any additions to your collection.

In fact, to be very brave, you can announce you are trimming the collection. Just like tree trimming, you are going to be doing some pruning and weeding and getting the collection down to a manageable size.

Then release to the universe ones that do not absolutely sing to you.

Donate them to a charity that you love and admire.

If you do not have space to display what remains, rotate three or four times a year so you have the chance to admire the ones that are worthy of your time and energy.

36. The Craft Room
(Not the Cr _ _ Room!)

The ability to simplify means to eliminate the unnecessary
so that the necessary may speak.

Hans Hofmann

A client hired me to put her house back together after a remodel. This was an important change for the family, as they had recently experienced the death of her husband at a young age. Not only was she grieving but so were her children. The remodel became a new beginning, a fresh start, a much-needed clean slate for all.

We worked for several days clearing clutter from the bedrooms and living spaces when she mentioned there was one additional room—the craft room. However, when she showed it to me she explained she had a more appropriate term for the space as it was literally filled up to the top with stuff. She had not been able to work in it for years but now she was ready.

We scheduled a return trip to focus on just that space. Before we started I asked her to sit with me in the newly redone and Zen-like space of her living room, away from all the crafts. Since we hadn't been able to navigate the craft room before, I asked my client to describe the various crafts she had in there.

She identified not one, not two, but at least three different kinds of crafts that were in the room. The client went on to share her level of interest in each and when she had worked on them before. As she talked I could see her energy level change from enthusiastic and excited to sadness as she shared with me about each craft.

I asked if she was ready to let go of one or two of the crafts, and focus on one that really interested her. She felt she was. She recognized that her craft space could not hold all of the materials she had purchased to pursue all three different crafts. She really wanted herself in the room, working and focusing on her hobbies, which she really enjoyed and had missed.

It turns out that a lot of the yarn purchases and products to go with knitting were made when her husband was ill. She showed me different knitting projects that she had started while she waited in various doctors' offices and hospital rooms. She said this gave her something to do with her hands. Within a split second of picking up the beginnings of a yarn project, she was taken right back to that moment and what was being said to her husband, how he was feeling, and how she felt.

She said she was ready to let the incompleteness of all of that go to others who could use her purchases.

This chaotically compressed container had been full to bursting and inaccessible when our team started de-cluttering. But several hours later, with much releasing and donating to others, we were able to get to the bones of the room. Next we planned out the space so it would be workable for my client. Then, in an organized, orderly fashion we put back the furniture and craft materials that would serve the client going forward.

Donations of materials the client was no longer going to use, especially the many skeins of yarn, were a much-needed release for her. A local women's shelter was thrilled to receive her donations, and she felt relief and a sense of freedom by letting go of painful memories of that time.

She was ready to move toward new beginnings and crafts that really excited her.

37. Go for a "Photo Finish"

Someday is not a day of the week.

UNKNOWN

Have you been saying that someday you'll get those photos organized? Yet, somehow with each day you have other things to do, other places to go, and other people to meet. So someday never arrives.

If you have been overwhelmed with photos here are some easy suggestions:

DIGITAL PHOTOS

Let's use the S.T.E.P.S.™ to clearing clutter mentioned at the end of Part One:

S: **Survey** the situation. Where are all the photos? Are they all on your phone? Are they still on your camera? Are they on various computers? Gather them into one location; get them off of your camera(s) and your phone and onto one computer. Look at backing up your photo files on an external drive and store it in another location outside your home or office.

T: **Toss** the trashy ones quickly—the blurry, the bad and the "I can't remember why I took that" pictures. Use that great "delete" button. If you have lots and lots to delete, just set a weekly goal and start separating the good from the bad and ugly.

E: **Examine** how you've been storing your digital photos. Has it been easy or extremely difficult to locate some events and pictures? Can you set up folders in chronological order?

YYYYMMDD—put the year first, then the month, followed by the date, for starters. Some folks like to get even more specific; it really depends on the individual and how you plan to use your photos.

P: **Plan** how you want to use them. Perhaps you want to create a running slide show on your computer or television screen.

Maybe you want to have several frames of digital photos in your home. There may be some special events you want to create albums for, such as baby's first year, special anniversary, a wonderful wedding, or a memorable vacation.

S: **Start** with which event is most important to you right now. If you could only organize one specific milestone, which one would it be? Once you answer that question you have a clear starting point. Schedule time in your calendar/planner to work on this.

Don't stress about all of it. Just decide where to begin and schedule time in your calendar when you will work on this. Make an appointment with yourself as to when it makes sense for this project to begin.

PRINTED PHOTOS

What if you have bags and bags and shoeboxes of old, printed photos?

Using the same steps as above. Go and find all those photos. Are some in the garage? Under the bed? On the floor of the hall closet? At the bottom of a junk drawer?

Gather them all into one room and survey the situation. Are you overwhelmed with the mountains of material? You may need to recruit some helpers for this one, depending on the amount of photos you have.

In your home which room or place can you put all of these?

_____

Who could you get to help?

_____

Do you have photo-safe, acid-free boxes available to get going with sorting the photos quickly? If not, get these before beginning. The task is to get them out of paper bags, plastic bags, or old cardboard boxes, and get the photos standing up in photo-safe, acid-free boxes and grouped into broad categories.

Grab a bag and start sorting. Using dividers in your photo boxes to separate different groupings, turn on some motivating music and get going. Be sure and have a handy "toss" bag to unload the blurry and the bad. Now is your chance to get rid of any photos that are not showing your best side!

Chances are there will be similarities in some of the containers. For example, one bag could have graduation pictures. Stand all graduation photos from that special day in the photo storing box. Just getting your photos in stand-up, soldier position, instead of flat, fallen-down sleeping slugs, will help you see them.

When you come to photos that are of something else entirely, take a divider and write that event, such as "Colorado summer vacation," and stand those pics in the box.

Stay focused for at least one to two hours so that you can see you are making headway.

Reward yourself for starting on this project and schedule when you will continue.

How do you eat an elephant? One bite at a time.

Once you have your "keepers" all in acid-free photo boxes, decide if there are a few memorable moments or special people that are worthy of being featured in an album. Not every picture is going in an album. Selecting the spectacular and the sentimental ones will help you decide which ones are "album worthy." This will be so much easier to do now, instead of from inside a paper bag!

38. Storage Units = Delayed Decisions

Indecision becomes decision with time.

UNKNOWN

Several clients have hired my team to clear clutter and empty their storage units. These are always interesting spaces, as one often does not know what all is in there. My husband and I used to own storage units, and I was always fascinated by the variety of reasons people rented those places.

According to the Self Storage Association International, there were nearly 50,000 self-storage facilities in the United States as of mid-2012. Compare that number to 1984, when there were only 6,600 units across the country.

One in 10 U.S. households currently rents a self-storage unit. That is an increase of 65% from just 15 years ago.

Are you one of the many paying monthly rent on items you haven't seen or used for quite some time? Have you ever sat down and added up the amount of money you have given to the storage facility to babysit your precious possessions?

Stop right now, and get out your calculator and storage agreement.

How many years? _____

How much per month? _____

Now multiply the number of months your items have been stored and put that total here:

_____

When was the last time you visited your storage items?

_____

Can you think of any future use for the money you could save by facing the storage unit with confidence, identifying what key items of value are in there, and deciding where those items could and should live?

There are various reasons for renting these units. Here are some I've heard: We just need it for a little while, until we get settled. I'm downsizing and I won't have room for all my things. I'll just put them in storage for a bit. We were moving and didn't have room to take everything. We thought we'd go back and take care of it but never did. My adult children haven't had time to go through their things from childhood, and I couldn't throw the items out without them looking at them.

If you must have a storage unit, install shelving and organize the space for easy access. Create a road map and inventory list so you know where items are located. Label the outside of any boxes and use clear containers when possible.

Storage unit de-cluttering by oneself is absolutely daunting and could be downright dangerous. You don't want to be inside a storage unit alone when a large piece of furniture or heavy box comes tumbling down on you. This de-cluttering calls for a team.

Think about the contents of your storage unit. If items in it belong to other people, have an authentic conversation with them about de-cluttering and develop a plan and process for addressing this within the next 12 months, if not sooner.

Be honest with them, but firm. If the majority of items belong to them, and you have been sharing the space, and they are unwilling to schedule time to address the unit, give them a deadline, telling them when you will be processing and removing your items.

Work with the management of the facility and get your name and billing information off of the unit as soon as possible.

39. The "Get Real" Reality:
We Aren't Taking the Stuff with Us When We Go – The Inevitable Last Stop

Things do not change; we change.

Henry David Thoreau

Have you given any thought to the fact that none of us is getting out of here alive? I know that's a pretty serious statement, but I dare anyone to tell me it's not true.

No matter how much we kick and scream, or go quietly in the night, there isn't a person among us who gets to take their possessions—the good, the bad, and the ugly—along for the ride to their next stop.

If you've ever been left with the task of closing out a family member's home, regardless of how big or small, you know how tough a job that can be. Don't wait until an illness or accident prevents you from clearing out and organizing the items in your life that are truly special and significant.

Now is the time to get real and get started. Start looking at your home through the lens of an outsider and see what's clogged up.

A client of mine had volunteered to empty a small apartment for a friend who had died. She had offered to the family that she would continue paying the rent, and would go through all of the items carefully and dispose of all the possessions in a gentle manner. This busy professional had a packed schedule and her own life to lead, so this task kept getting postponed, until one day when she called me.

Her opening words to me were, "Do you help people on overwhelm?" She had tried to do this task by herself, and each time she went to the space to begin she was overcome with grief and bewilderment. It was too much for one person alone to go through boxes, make decisions, make arrangements to dispose of various items, and close down the rental.

Together we were able to empty the space, get special items to family members, donate other possessions, and end the rental fees for her. While this was a difficult task for my client, she was so relieved to complete the assignment and get on with living her own life.

What plan do you have in place for your possessions?

If you have several family members, now is the time to give them the opportunity to discuss and agree on distribution.

When could you have these conversations?

Who will you include?

---

40. There's No Place Like Home:
Creating Your Ideal Home

Home is where the heart is.

PLINY THE ELDER

Dorothy really did have it right: There is no place like home. If ours is not ideal right now, what can we do about it? One thing for sure is we shouldn't waste a lot of time dwelling on what we don't have at the moment—whether that's not enough room or not the right furniture or that the floors are all wrong.

We could end up spending a lot of energy focusing on what's missing. Instead, I propose concentrating on what is and what you do have control over.

Our homes are what we make them. If we make them too full and bursting, we run out of air to breathe, and room to create and recreate. Maybe some parts aren't perfect, but then we, also, have flaws, so can we find what works and capitalize on that?

There must have been some things about the place where we are living that we liked, or we wouldn't have chosen it. Just like a long-term relationship, it's important to review all of its good points, and build from there.

This place may not be ideal, but think quietly about what small changes could you make to make it more of a haven than it is.

Let's not waste any more time recalling days of where we used to live or dreaming of where we hope to live someday. We have the gift of the present. What could we do to make our current situation better?

Clearing up obvious clutter

Bringing down the volume of the visual noise

Lightening up our load and letting go

Sorting what we really love and need

Finding homes for our possessions

Letting everyone in our household know where that home is

Getting everything in its place

Remember to label, label, label when you can so no one has to remember where items live.

Stop complaining if the home does not stay clean. A home can't get cleaned if there is too much clutter. Clear up the clutter first so that you or someone else can clean next.

Remember: You can't clean what's cluttered!

Get ready for the cleaning lady, even if that's *you!*

Part Three: BUSINESS

41. My King of Focus

The key to success is to focus our conscious mind on things we desire, not things we fear.

BRIAN TRACY

We live in a constant age of distraction. There are so many ways to get off task; it really boggles the mind how many. It's amazing any of us get anything accomplished anymore.

Way back in the last century when everyone's phone was a landline, we could go out into the world and handle life "on the outside." When we returned to our office or home we'd check our answering machine to see who called and give them a call back. Calls came in through landlines and, unless the place was burning, often those calls went to voice mail or someone took a message.

Then along came e-mails, cell phones, smartphones, call forwarding, ways to run our businesses remotely, Skype, YouTube, internet surfing, Facebook, Twitter and Instagram—to name some of the ways we can get distracted.

Many of us boast about our multitasking techniques—how we can keep more balls in the air than any circus juggler. It's really nothing to be proud of because it really does limit our efficiency.

Let's take a look at who I call "The King of Focus": Captain Sully Sullenberger.

You may be thinking right now that the name sounds familiar but you just can't quite place it. Here's a refresher:

Captain Sullenberger was the pilot of the US Airways jet flying over Manhattan on January 15, 2009, who discovered his plane had lost not one but both engines because birds had gotten stuck in the engines. He had less than two minutes to focus and concentrate on how to safely land the commercial plane with 155 lives on board.

What he did in a brief amount of time became referred to as "The Miracle on the Hudson." Captain Sullenberger didn't wander about the plane asking people for ideas about what to do. He didn't start looking at all the open field space in New Jersey, just across the Hudson River. He didn't begin a research project on where other landing strips were.

Captain Sullenberger stayed the course and stayed focused on creating the best possible outcome for all the passengers and crew.

He was not driven by fear; instead, he put his expertise, training, and *conscious mind* into the task in front of him. With Captain Sullenberger's concentration, he and all those aboard that day lived to tell family and friends about that miraculous day of focus.

We've been living in the age of distraction, as Leo Babauta so aptly calls it in his great little book, *Focus: A Simplicity Manifesto in the Age of Distraction.* We are overloaded with information and so much is coming at us from all angles. We are drowning in the many temptations for our attention, so in order to stay above water we get on our hamster wheel of multitasking behavior, trying desperately to keep up.

We boast about how busy we are and how we are master multitaskers, but the research doesn't back up that this is an efficient technique for getting things done. *The Wall Street Journal* reported that only 2.5% of people can multitask efficiently, while many more folks *think* they can.

Those people are really switching back and forth, as noted cognitive scientist David Meyer of the University of Michigan has reported. He states that multitasking is becoming more prevalent, but that it is "very often highly inefficient and can be dangerous to your health."

Meyer states that humans can't do two cognitively complicated tasks at once because there is only one mental and neural channel through which language flows, and that we have distinct bandwidth challenges, making it difficult for our brains to process information. Depending on the complexity of the tasks, Meyer reports that it can take 50% more time or longer when people try to complete two or more tasks at once.

According to researchers at the University of Utah, even driving the car while using a hands-free device makes us just as impaired as if we are holding the phone. It's not the device; it's the fact that we are using the language channel to speak, plan our next move, and read the road signs, all at the same time. According to Melinda Beck at *The Wall Street Journal,* drivers talking on cell phones are four times as likely to get into traffic accidents as those who aren't.
In what areas do you need better focus?

Why haven't you given those areas the focus they deserve?

_____

What excuses have you been using as to why you've not focused?

_____

If you were to restructure your daily schedule, how could you create blocks of focused time?

_____

When could you begin that?

_____

What project(s) have you been avoiding that you could begin?

_____

_____

42. Your Cockpit Is Your Command Center

It is not enough if you are busy.
The question is what are you busy about.

HENRY DAVID THOREAU

Where is your cockpit? What's that, you say? You don't have a plane. No plane is necessary. We are all pilots of our own lives, so let's get your life back on the right course.

Whether you have a business or not, we are all in the business of living our best lives, but sometimes those lives get off track. That's when we need to put on our captain's cap and take charge, just like Sully Sullenberger did in 2009 before landing his US Airways jet on the Hudson River successfully.

You might be CEO of a large corporation or CEO of a small family or someone somewhere in between. No matter the size of the operation, it's important to have your tools of the trade within arm's reach.

For the busy CEO parent this cockpit might be an area in the kitchen where the family schedules and carpool calendars, along with the school papers that need signing, are kept. In other words, you need a command center.

For those without young ones at home you might designate an area you enjoy working in and completing the tasks and business of daily living: computer station, tickler file, action files, and contact info.

If you have a separate room in your home that you can use, create a home office space with your cockpit. Whether you have a home office or an office outside the home, a command center is crucial to your success.

Important ingredients for success:

Good lighting

Great ergonomic chair and ergonomic keyboard

Minimum distractions

Also: computer, printer, shredder, recycling bin, trash can, stapler, staple remover, file drawers, writing instruments, file folders, reference

materials, hanging files.
Add what else you need here:

Think about your CEO responsibilities. What materials do you need close at hand, within arm's reach or an easy swivel of your chair, for you to be so focused that success is not only probable but almost guaranteed?

Creating Your Own Command Center

Materials needed: About 10-12 hanging file folders, a wire mesh or cardboard desktop file organizer (the cardboard ones with the lid give a quiet place for papers but only work if you open and process them!), a daily/monthly sorter available at your local office supply store, your current active pieces of paper, and tabs to make the following files:

Action, Awaiting Reply, Bills to Pay, Calls to Make, Data Entry, Do it Now (2 minutes or less), E-mails to Send, Someday/Maybe, To File, To Read

HOW IT WORKS:

Place each labeled hanging file folder in the desktop organizer in the order above (which happens to be alphabetical). Add folders for any important people you meet with regularly.

Grab your stack of papers and get them all facing one way, making it easy for you to read them quickly.

Set a timer and see if within 30 minutes all those loose papers can be sorted into one of those categories.

Voila! You have taken command of your papers and taken back control.

Now as the captain it is up to you to oversee these files by opening one or two folders each day and seeing what needs to be done. Items to discuss with certain individuals will be in that person's folder. The captain needs to schedule a time to meet with others and discuss and resolve topics in a timely manner.

The secret here is twofold: 1. opening one or two file folders daily, and 2. taking action on the contents.

Think like Captain Sullenberger and take action.

The miracle on the Hudson would not have happened had he not taken command!

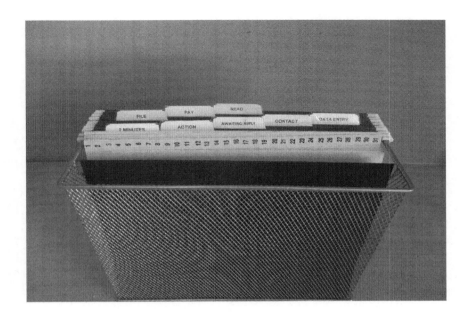

Command Center

43. Clear the ~~Decks~~ Desks

Happiness is a very small desk and a very big wastebasket.

ROBERT ORBEN

It's sit-down time, or what I lovingly refer to as BIC (butt in chair!) time. You are ready to get serious about a big project you're working on. You've got deadlines looming like incoming storm clouds. You've got so many burners going and responsibilities lurking around every corner, you don't know which way to turn.

This is the perfect time to clear your ~~cockpit~~ work space.

Take a look at it right now. Is it covered with so many papers, projects, and piles that keeping track of what's where and which one to do next are making you think about escaping to a desert isle, if only you could remember which pile has that cool brochure?

Ask yourself: What is the best use of my time right now? In other words, look at your next block of time and ask: What is my highest priority?

That's the project to put front and center (or off to one side of your computer), and that's the only project that should remain on your desk.

Put all the others in a drawer marked "next," in a file drawer marked "ongoing projects," on a console table behind you, or—last resort—on the floor.

In other words you are clearing the desk for high focus, high concentration, high efficiency, and letting your brain drill into that one best thing to work on.

I'm not saying to pitch all the other pressing projects. Just get them out of your visual screen and give your mind time for clarity, creativity, and calm. With these three Cs, your project at hand has a greater chance of completion than before you cleared the desk.

Productivity expert and author David Allen wrote that projects are those activities that take more than one action step. The key to not feeling so cluttered in our minds about all we need to accomplish is to keep those projects moving forward. We should continuously ask ourselves what's the next logical action needed to keep this moving: a phone call to make, an e-mail, some research, writing a report or a review, or setting up a meeting.

Whatever it is, the key is to keep it moving—whatever the "it" is for you.

There's no need to keep 10–20 piles on your desk to show how busy and important your job is. This is not a contest to see who has the most or highest piles of paper.

It's keeping your desk clear for creative thought and productivity. Then, instead of sinking with your ship, you can sail right through any storm and arrive safely at the next port!

44. Drowning in Paper?
Get R _ _ _ _!

You drown not by falling into a river,
but by staying submerged in it.

PAULO COEHLO

AccORDING to statistics from the National Association of Professional Organizers (NAPO), 80% of the papers we keep we don't really use or need. Getting to a paperless society was discussed as early as the 1970s, yet many of us are drowning in more paper now than ever.

Printers have become much smaller and so convenient to use. Besides at work, printers are in most homes across the country. For some, when left with uncertainty, the thought becomes, "I'll just print a copy."

We've also become a litigious society so we tell ourselves we better make sure we have a copy, "just in case."

Then, with identity theft on the rise, we rationalize it's better not to throw those papers out anyway.

Not everyone is suffering from this drowning. Some companies and some families have gone paperless and have placed files in secured, cloud-based programs.

But not everyone.

For those not yet ready to make the leap, here are some suggestions:

1. Gather the loose papers in your business or home.

2. Get six banker's boxes from the local office supply store. If you have a lot of paper you may need to triple this number to 18.

3. Label the first five as follows: **R**eading, **A**ction, **F**ile, **T**oss/ recycle, and **S**hred = **R.A.F.T.S.**™

4. Set a designated time on your calendar. Put on your favorite dancing music and get moving.

5. Pick up a stack of your papers that are about an inch or two thick. Flip through them and get them all facing the right way, so you won't have to stand on your head to read them.

Square up the corners so they are in a neat stack. Now *quickly with each paper* decide: Is this something to **read?** Drop it in the read box. Something that requires **action?** Drop it in the action box. Do not stop to work on it now. You are doing a quick sort first.

6. Is it something you have already handled, but you are needing to file it? Drop it in the box marked **file.**

7. Next use the box marked **toss/recycle.** Be sure if anything has confidential information that you put it in the **shred** box.

8. Put the lids on the boxes. Congratulate yourself for processing a bunch of paper.

9. Schedule another block of time as soon as possible to process the action box first.

10. Open the **action** box. Take the items out of that box. Divide the items into: **2 minutes or less, deadline-driven,** or **action—other.** Make a folder for each—or better yet, use your command center files you set up in Chapter 42.

11. Schedule a time in your calendar as soon as possible to address the action group, especially the deadline-driven ones.

12. New day—open the **read** box.

13. Set up a second **read** box.

14. Mark the first one "**business**" and the second one "**pleasure.**"

15. Empty the **read** box from the first day, and very quickly sort all of the reading material into one of those two categories.

If you have no filing system or have one that has not been serving you well, you may want to check out FreedomFiler™ (www. FreedomFiler.com), a self-purging filing solution for home and office. This clever company was founded in 2001 by Seth Odam of San Diego. If you have been dealing with paper pain for too long, this product is worth investigating.

Over the years I've used a variety of filing systems but have found the FreedomFiler Home Filing Kit the best paper flow system available. As a certified FreedomFiler consultant I have seen firsthand how this product helps individuals and households take back control of their papers.

The kit retails for less than $35 and has pre-printed, adhesive labels that are color-coded by category for ease of filing: permanent, tax-related, policies, active, and reference.

There are additional blank labels so the product can be individualized for a particular situation.

To put this system together you need boxes of hanging file folders and clear plastic tabs, along with the kit itself. Easy, step-by-step directions are included with each kit.

The FreedomFiler Home Filing Kit can be ordered online at www.freedomfiler.com/RED.

FreedomFiler Home Filing Kit

45. Prioritization, Not Perfection

Done is better than perfect.

MARK LeBLANC

Guess what? It's not "he who dies with the most items on his to-do list wins." There's no prize for that other than probably dropping dead of exhaustion, worry, fatigue, and feeing like a failure.

When we leave this world for another there will still be things left in our "inbox of life" that we did not complete. Is that news shocking to you? If so, take a few minutes and reflect on that. Do you have a written wish list, a Goals 101, or bucket list? If not, now is the time to get those dreams, ideas, aspirations, and visions down in written form.

Are you wasting some days on busyness or using those tasks to rationalize that you can't get on with what *you* want to do because of other people's priorities?

Do you postpone starting a project because you keep searching for the perfect place to put that in your calendar and you can't find any blank spots? Are work responsibilities eating up your energy, your enthusiasm, and your effervescence?

Is everything just running around in your head, and you feel like your brain could burst with all you are trying to remember?

Now is the time to stop all of that.

Create a "master list" today and give your brain a break:

1. One master list if you don't have a business life and a personal life, or

2. One master list divided into two parts: business and personal.

This list can be kept in various forms. You decide where will work for you. The master to-do list can be on your smartphone, in a computer folder, in a manila file, in a small notebook, or in some kind of planner/calendar system.

If you've had a to-do list for years but have found you never got around to doing the things on there, this time make it a "will-do list" and put on the list things you *will* do.

Where you keep it is very personal to your own learning style. Build on what has worked for you in the past. The important thing here is to get it out of your head and relieve the stress of trying to remember everything.

As Jim Temme wrote, "The key is not to prioritize what's on your schedule, but to schedule your priorities."

Always, always ask yourself: what is the best use of my time, right now?

When is your most productive time of the day? Is it early morning before the house, town and telephone are awake? Is it mid-morning? Is it late at night when the world starts to shut down for the day? Whatever time is your best time, schedule the tasks that take creative thought and concentration. Save the simpler tasks for other times of the day or, better yet, delegate or dump them.

46. Backward Map Your Projects

If you don't know where you're going, any road will get you there.

LEWIS CARROLL

Stephen Covey said it so well in his book, *The 7 Habits of Highly Effective People*, "Begin with the end in mind." I call this backward mapping—getting a clear picture of what does completion look like.

For any and all of our projects we should be able to visualize the end point—the goal. The more specific and clear we can be about it, the better our backward map can be.

If we don't know where we're going, any road will get us there, so it's important to build a road map starting with the end in mind.

Projects are different from tasks. Tasks might require a single step—just something we need to do or schedule when we will do it.

There are several steps with projects; often they involve others and are more complex. They require strategizing, planning, and creative thought.

One way to do this is by making a mind map. Draw a two-inch circle in the center of a blank paper and write your end goal in the center. Draw several straight lines out from the circle. This might be seven or more, depending on the complexity of the project.

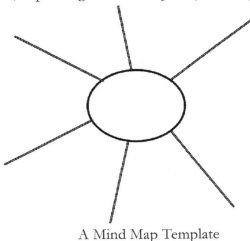

A Mind Map Template

Think of specific steps that need to be taken to reach that goal you wrote in the center, and write each step on one of the lines.

Keep brainstorming and adding to the mind map names of people who might help, resources you will need to get, and anything tied to reaching the end point.

Don't worry about the sequence of steps at this phase; just get the ideas out of your head.

There are mind mapping tools available online if you prefer.

Tony Buzan is the inventor of mind mapping. Visit www. ThinkBuzan.com for specific mind mapping tools developed by him and his company. There is a free mind mapping software on this site as well as ones for purchase.

Other sites to visit for mind mapping are www.TheBrain.com and www.MindMeister.com. More companies are developing mind map software all the time, so continue to check the web for newer products and versions.

This is such a creative way to think and brainstorm ideas, either on your own or with others for group projects. Add color and specificity so the entire project and the very best sequence of steps can be identified. Then, chunk big projects into bite-sized bits and keep asking: What's the next action to move this project forward?

47. The Big "Ds":
Dump—Delegate—Do—Defer

Success is the sum of small efforts,
repeated day in and day out.

ROBERT COLLIER

When faced with work tasks there are only certain things we can do with them. I call these the "D List":

Dump—Delegate—Do—or Defer

DUMP: Asking ourselves if this assignment needs to be done is always an important question. If we are busy doing work-related assignments, but not productive, these items can probably be dumped, if not delegated to someone else.

What's important here is finding out why we are over here fooling around with busy items instead of productive ones. Do we not want to get started on something that appears difficult, so we have gravitated to something simple instead? Are we in a job or career that doesn't feed our soul so we get side-tracked and unproductive? He who has the longest to-do list does not win, so take a look and start eliminating items so that the list goes from the many to the few.

If we ask ourselves, "What are the big rocks here?" we are getting at the essence. In other words, what's the essential work to do? What are activities of high importance and value?

Dump everything else. It doesn't mean the task or project is dumped forever, though it could be. Great ideas and wonderful projects can be placed in a "someday/maybe" file for personal goals and a "later" file for business. Taking this step is important so your ideas don't get lost forever. Take a few minutes to mind map any specifics about the idea so those are captured but cleared out of your mind, making room for working and living in the present.

DELEGATE: For some of us this is a difficult one. It's hard to let go of pieces of a project. We think that no one will do it exactly the way we would. And you know what? That's true. The key questions here are: Am I the best one to do this? Is this the best use of my time? What's my time worth? Am I spending time on tasks or projects that I do well, or am I spending time on tasks I don't do well or don't enjoy and that someone else could do so much better?

By delegating some tasks we are freed up to focus and concentrate on our strength areas and relax and release other components. What's important is being very clear about our directions and expectations, and checking back with the individual to clarify and give support.

DO: As Nike says, "Just Do It." If we just get in and begin, often we find out the task was not as painful or as difficult as we first thought. Can we get in and just take the first bite, the first step, the first action, to get it started?

DEFER: Maybe this work assignment or project is perfect for you but maybe not at this time. Evaluate whether you have the authority and the availability to move this project to a time that makes more sense for you and the company. Have the deadlines for this assignment been set in stone or is there a possibility of flexibility? These key questions can help you decide the next best steps.

48. Batch to the Max

Don't fit the task into your schedule; rather schedule tasks into designated blocks of time.

SUE CRUM

This has nothing to do with a batch of cookies. Instead, I'm talking about batching like tasks with like. How does this work? Rather than switching back and forth among a variety of tasks, batch similar ones together, when possible. Earlier I mentioned about when you're out, work to be out and get several outside events or tasks taken care of during that time frame.

The "batch to the max" proposal is somewhat similar, yet different. For example, schedule certain times during the day to check e-mail rather than having e-mails dictate and direct your day. When you need to make or return phone calls, complete several and leave a voice message stating when a good time would be to reach you. In other words, state something like, "I'm catching up on my phone calls this afternoon. Please call me back at your earliest convenience, and if this afternoon isn't a good time for us to connect, please leave some times when we can talk."

If you are in need of creative time and planning time, look at your schedule and see when you can batch some blocks of 30–45 minutes or more so that you can get the creative juices flowing with the absolute least amount of interruptions possible.

For those in office environments it may need to be before others arrive at work or after most have gone home. Is there a small empty space you can retreat to for 30 minutes of uninterrupted time? Not all jobs have this. Just think about where and how you can schedule planning and think time into your day. The creative mind needs time to ponder profoundly, think quietly, and produce. This cannot be accomplished at a high level if one is switching tasks throughout the day.

Some people boast of their multitasking abilities, yet it's nothing to boast about. It's really switch-tasking and, in the long run, not as productive as concentrated focus on one kind of activity.

If you can own your schedule somewhat, view it with a new, critical eye. Look ahead to the next month, as the one you're probably in has you going from here to there and everywhere in between. If you have been frustrated because you haven't been able to get to any long-term strategic planning or developing that key presentation or writing that new business plan, see if you can find some blocks of time for creating those, and calendar a date or two for yourself.

Then when someone starts asking about a meeting with you on a date you have a creative block of time with that important person (you), work to find a different date and protect your thinking block of time from being eroded.

If you own your own business, especially if you are a solopreneur, you recognize there are many hats you wear. See if you can batch as many similar activities together as possible. There is a need for administrative tasks when one is the sole proprietor. Batch those activities together and get them done in short order, or use a virtual assistant if you can. What's important is getting yourself back to your core business and taking care of your current customers while attracting new ones.

49. Are You in Business or in Hobby?

Once you find something you love to do, be the best at doing it.

DEBBI FIELDS

According to Intuit Small Business, the chance of a small business failing within five years is 49% and surviving at least seven years is only 31%.

It seems everywhere you go conversations often turn to someone who's just started a business to another person who is simply exploring the possibility.

Often, a business idea evolves from something we enjoy doing. We start to think perhaps this could become a business. A friend or relative might say, "Oh, you'd be smart to take that product or skill and start a business."

But would you?

Could you?

Do you have the time, the talent, and the tenacity to be successful right now?

Or should you just keep this interest as a hobby?

There's absolutely nothing wrong with hobbies. We all need them. Our brains deserve a chance to focus in a different direction every once in a while.

If you decide to go into business it's important to put some structure around your schedule. Sometimes people want to do something part-time to see if it is a business they want to pursue. Others need to have several other sources of income while a new business gets underway.

There is a cost to starting a business. Check with your local community regarding a business license, business insurance, requirements, and startup costs.

Don't think that having your own business will give you more time with your family; it will be just the opposite, especially in the beginning phases.

The United States Small Business Administration (SBA) has a wealth of information for anyone thinking about starting or for those already in business. Visit www.sba.gov.

Another wonderful resource for business owners is www.Score.

121

org. This nonprofit association has been helping small businesses for almost 50 years with more than 340 Score chapters across the country. Their work has been supported by the SBA, offering free mentoring from volunteer experts, inexpensive or free business workshops, and free online tools.

As Michael Gerber states in his book *The E-Myth Revisited*, it's important to understand it's not just about being passionate about what you do. One has to get the operations side of the business in place, such as financing, marketing, customer data, and sufficient capital, including not only starting but staying in business.

50. Technology as a Tool, Not a Tether

There are managers so preoccupied with their e-mail messages that they never look up from their screens to see what's happening in the non-digital world.

MIHALY CSIKSZENTMIHALYI

There's no turning back. We are in the 21st century, with all the technology tools and tidbits that our parents and grandparents never imagined. The world is really a much different place today. In many ways technology has made the world easier to navigate, communicate, and investigate. The wide world of the web has made so many things feel much easier and close at hand.

When it's all working, we feel on top of the world. We are humming and getting things done fast! We can't imagine going back to the old ways of doing certain tasks.

Having so many technology tools at our fingertips should be helping make our lives easier, and less stressed. Yet, somehow, for many of us these things are adding emotional mayhem to our lives and schedules.

Learning new tools can take some time and focus. While some of us are earlier adopters to the latest and greatest, others need concentrated time and attention from patient teachers, and opportunities for mass practice with new tech tools. By mass practice I mean repetition in the beginning to create an almost automatic use of the technology, like muscle memory. For late adopters showing them a new tool and expecting immediate total comprehension and implementation sets them up for failure.

Whether you are an early adopter or a late one, it's important to give our bodies and minds some breaks from technology from time to time. Unplug for a while and get outside in the fresh air. Talking to people in person and taking in our surroundings can be refreshing and rejuvenating. Turning off a cell phone or, better yet, leaving it behind when getting out in nature can help all of us to breathe deeper and slower, and more calmly. See if untethering for a bit and getting a different view of the world helps to clear the clutter in your mind and open you to new experiences and breathing space.

Love the one you're with.

STEPHEN STILLS

123

Final Thoughts

Success is not mere achievement, but rather the more difficult feat of handling your life efficiently. It means to be a success as a person, controlled, organized, not part of the world's problems, but part of its cure.

NORMAN VINCENT PEALE

This book would not be complete without mentioning that sometimes we need to de-clutter not only things, activities, and places, but people from our lives.

For many this is a very difficult issue. If your journey to clearing up the clutter in your life is not complete because of certain individuals or groups of people, now is maybe the time to address that. Think of the people in your life and whether or not they fill your vessel, uplift you, and make your heart sing—or do they drain you and wear you out with exhaustion?

Seek out more time with those who are positive, and put a boundary around the time you spend thinking about or being with negative-energy folks. If this continues to be a difficult area for you to de-clutter, seek counseling from a qualified, licensed therapist.

When you find *yourself* with negative self-talk, stop immediately, catch yourself. Then, refocus and regroup your thoughts to something positive.

As I mentioned at the beginning, this book is intended to be a guide, and no one needs to read the chapters in order if they don't want. Find the ones that speak directly to you and start there.

Think of this book as a smorgasbord. You probably don't need 50 different helpings to get on with clearing your clutter. Which ones really resonate with you?

Start there and start small.

The important thing is that you start. Take action. Visualize your success in small doses and reward yourself along the way.

Remember to ask for help with the larger projects.

Keep it all moving, whatever "it" means to you.

This is your one life.

The world is a cluttered place.

Now is the time to de-clutter yours.

I love to hear people's success stories and would enjoy hearing yours. Please send those to me at Sue@ClearYourClutterCoach.com.

Clutter-clearing and organizing one's life is a process, not a one-day event. By continuing to clutter-clear and assign homes for the things and activities you want in your life, you will create a calmer, less-stressful lifestyle. This will take commitment on your part, but it is worth the effort.

Living with less stress and clutter-free will create breathing room for you to have more happiness and get on with the life you want and deserve.

It is worth the effort.

It's time now to take your fork and dig in!

Additional Resources
ASSOCIATIONS

www.appo.org—Association of Personal Photo Organizers (APPO)

www.challengingdisorganization.org—Institute for Challenging Disorganization (ICD), formerly the National Study Group on Chronic Disorganization (NSGCD)

www.napo.net—National Association of Professional Organizers (NAPO); look for local chapters in your area

www.nasmm.org—National Association of Senior Move Managers (NASMM)

www.organizersincanada.com—Professional Organizers in Canada (POC)

www.aapo.org.au—The Australasian Association of Professional Organisers (AAPO)

BOOKS: The Top 10 Favorites for Clearing Your Clutter

Allen, David. *Getting Things Done: The Art of Stress-Free Productivity*

Babauta, Leo. *Focus: A Simplicity Manifesto in the Age of Distraction*

Canfield, Jack. *The Success Principles: How to Get From Where You Are to Where You Want to Be*

Covey, Stephen. *The 7 Habits of Highly Effective People*

Gerber, Michael E. *The E Myth Revisited: Why Most Small Businesses Don't Work and What to Do About It*

Hagen, Elizabeth. *Organize with Confidence*

Koch, Richard. *The 80/20 Principle: The Secret to Success by Achieving More with Less*

Rohrbach, Annie. *Conscious Order: Clear Your Mind, Leave Clutter Behind*

Tracy, Brian. *Eat That Frog!: 21 Great Ways to Stop Procrastination and Get More Done in Less Time*

Tracy, Brian. *Goals!: How to Get Everything You Want—Faster Than You Ever Thought Possible*

PLACES FOR DONATIONS

www.ClothingDonations.org—a service of Vietnam Veterans of America that picks up your used clothes or household goods and uses them to support Veterans' programs; call 1.888.518.VETS (8387).

www.DonateMyDress.org—looking for prom and sweet 16 dresses for girls who can't afford them.

www.DressForSuccess.org—looking for new or nearly new women's work clothes.

www.FoodPantries.org—look for food banks or soup kitchens near you.

www.Goodwill.org—Call 1.800.GOODWILL.

www.Habitat.org—Habitat for Humanity International.

www.ILoveSchools.org—Put in your zip code and find nearby schools that can use your unneeded supplies and children's books.

www.LovingHugs.org—accepts almost-new stuffed animals for children in orphanages, refugee camps, and war zones.

www.SalvationArmy.org—The Salvation Army.

www.Soles4Souls.org—looking for new and used shoes for distribution worldwide; enter your zip code to find a collection site near you.

www.svdpusa.org—Society of St. Vincent de Paul, Inc.

Donate blankets and towels to local animal shelters.

Donate books to local libraries.

Donate magazines to local hospitals and doctors' offices (remove your personal information first).

Donate also to your favorite charity of choice.

Release to the universe that which no longer meets your needs or that you want.

MORE RESOURCES

www.FreedomFiler.com/RED—self-purging, low-cost adhesive label system for paper management.

www.CatalogChoice.org—register to stop unwanted catalogs, coupons, credit card offers, and other junk mail that arrives daily.

www.dmachoice.org/index.php—additional resource for stopping the paper clutter from coming in.

www.DoNotCall.gov—National Do Not Call Registry; call 1.888.382.1222.

www.Earth911.org—provides earth-friendly ways to dispose of many difficult items.

www.Freecycle.org—helps connect people who have things to give away.

www.PlannerPads.com—has calendar/planning systems that can start at four different times of the year.

www.WorldPrivacyForum.org—see their recommended top-10 opt-out list.

RESOURCES SPECIFIC TO THE SAN DIEGO AREA

www.1800HaulOut.com—great haul-out team in central San Diego; may be able to drop off some donations, too.

www.ConsignmentClassics.net—takes furniture, art, and accessories in good condition; also accepts jewelry and clothing.

www.DinnerAtHome-sd.com—owner Pamela Croft is available to prepare specialized meals and deliver to you, plus catering services.

http://my.neighbor.org—Father Joe's Villages accepts many donations.

www.PC-Photo.net—professional photo lab, including conversion, restoration, and scanning.

www.RecycleSanDiego.org—free electronics recycling.

www.TotalSecureShredding.com—mobile shredding (comes to your home or office) as well as a main drop-off location.

www.wrcsd.org—Women's Resource Center, a place for women and their families who are in domestic violence situations, located in Oceanside; accepts donations of clothing not needing repair, and usable household, decorative and personal items.

NOTE: At the time of printing all the resources above were organizations or businesses in operation.

About the Author

Sue Crum, founder of ClearYourClutterCoach.com, has been helping people clear up their clutter and get on with the life they imagine and deserve for many years. She considers herself an accidental organizer, as she came to this work when her life was evolving and she was in need of regrouping and clearing clutter out of her own life. She discovered everyone has stuff and at some point in one's life, we end up with more stuff than we need.

Sue is past president of NAPO-San Diego (National Association of Professional Organizers) and is a Golden Circle member of NAPO-National. Besides her training in the professional organizing field, she is also an Accredited Staging Professional (ASP) and has helped hundreds of homeowners not only clear clutter from their homes, but in many cases stage them to sell or stage them to stay, after de-cluttering.

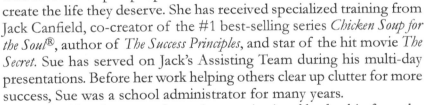

Sue is an international motivational speaker who loves to inspire people to take action and create the life they deserve. She has received specialized training from Jack Canfield, co-creator of the #1 best-selling series *Chicken Soup for the Soul*®, author of *The Success Principles*, and star of the hit movie *The Secret*. Sue has served on Jack's Assisting Team during his multi-day presentations. Before her work helping others clear up clutter for more success, Sue was a school administrator for many years.

She holds a doctorate degree in organizational leadership from the University of Southern California, a master's degree from California State University, Los Angeles, and a bachelor's degree from Bradley University in Peoria, Illinois.

After 21 winters in Illinois, Sue decided there might be better weather somewhere else! She bought her first car, a red convertible, at age 21, thanked her parents for raising her, and drove to Southern California, where ironically, she became a black diamond downhill skier with an annual season pass!

When she is not speaking or consulting, Sue can be found downhill skiing in the winter or boogie boarding at the beach in the summer. She feels blessed to live at the beach in San Diego County with her husband and dog from rescue.

Special Free Gift from the Author
FREE Organizing Package
Get Started Today!

- Free Quick Start Guide – *Simple Strategies for Clutter Clearing You Can Do Now!!*

Plus

- Free Newsletter – *Quick eTips News for Energized and Efficient People*

Go To
ClearYourClutterCoach.com

Sign Up Now